LINEAGE

LINEAGE

What if the Universe
Gave You a Gift?

Nancy Burson

ThankYouVeryMuch
PUBLISHING
New York

Third Edition
Copyright © 2006, 2007, 2008 by Nancy Burson

ThankYouVeryMuch Publishing
P.O. Box 60
Prince Street Station
New York, New York 10012
www.TYVMPublishing.com

Library of Congress Control Number
2007937741

ISBN: 978-0-615-19546-9

Editors: Judy Gitenstein, Ja-lene Clark, Sheila Lewis, Bernadette Luckett,
and Sherie Tucker
Front cover photo: Copyright © Mary Jo Kuehne/Nancy Burson
Cover Design: David Marty
Book design: Gilda Hannah
All Photographs copyright © Nancy Burson unless otherwise indicated.

Third Edition published March 2008

ACKNOWLEDGMENTS

My profound gratitude to all the teachers in my life: the humans, the Celestials, and the Extra Celestials.

To my dear Mr. Keir, my own lineage and Seir Kieran of inspiration. My deepest love and gratitude for this lifetime of learning.

Thanks to Judy Gitenstein and Ja-lene Clark who edited the complicated first passes at the manuscript, integrating all the material. Many thanks as well to Sheila Lewis, who added the finishing touches to the previous revision, and finally to Cherie Tucker and Bernadette Luckett who brilliantly edited this third edition of *Lineage*.

My gratitude to my friend and teacher, Derek O'Neill, the Avatar in my life—for two thousand years of wisdom guided by Love; Jodi Serota, whose profound gifts aligned with God to create significant pivotal moments in my life; Starr Fuentes for her friendship and guidance through the years; and Isabelle Kingston for endowing me with love for the lands of Merlin.

Many thanks to the thousand or so people who purchased the first and second editions of *Lineage*, supporting the story before it was complete.

Thanks and heartfelt gratitude to both Katie Kline and Kate Hurni, my multi-talented collaborators, who assisted in everything from graphics and photography, to the orchestration of Evening Presentations.

Thanks to Marc Serges and Sandra Zane from Global Literary Management, who welcomed me and nurtured me as well, and to Shira Dicker for introducing me to them.

Special thanks to Brian Clamp, who is fearless in his support of my art.

To Mindy Lutch and Rick Siegel, my loving niece and nephew who always show up, and to their friend Libby Birkenmeier, who introduced us all to glow-in-the-dark Mary.

My sincere gratitude to David Kramlich, my partner in parenting.

Many thanks to Michael Julian Berz, Steve Alexander, Stuart Dike, and Mary Jo Kuehne for their memorable photos of amazing moments, profound places, and loving Light Beings.

Special thanks to Meryl Beck for her consistent love and support in joining me in the fields of Wiltshire and elsewhere.

Thanks to Larry Dukhovny for his inventive technical support.

Loving gratitude to Victor Dyment, Kate McCallum, Linda Mitele, Barbara Reeder, MJ Sawyer, Brook Still, Helen Marien, and Bernadette Luckett for their healing friendships.

My gratitude to Gilda Hannah for her last-minute text design magic.

And to my dearest Rays, my Universe of authors, I extend the bluest of gratitude, for without you this book wouldn't be. You are my constant reminder to "Look at your life through heaven's eyes."

CONTENTS

INTRODUCTION

Lineage noun (lin-age, also lin-e-age)
The descendants of a common ancestry

Are we alone in this vast Universe? Does life exist on other planets or in other dimensions? If so, what do those beings look like? And what if ETs are an aspect of God?

I never questioned my core belief in God. My belief system had always been a part of my life from the time I was a little girl. "How is it that God works?" was the big question in my mind. Where does the Divine leave off and mankind begin? When I began to study metaphysics (the science of being and knowing), someone said to me, "Do you think that all souls come from the Earth?" That was a question to ponder. "Is it possible to see God?" was another one. I wanted proof, and the proof I wanted was to experience my own direct connection to the Universe.

I believe that my career as a photographer was divinely guided, as all our lives are. That path led me to photograph energy more than a decade ago. Since then, I have asked to do so in the highest energetic vortexes throughout the world, as well as in my own home and studio.

It's been many years now since I began to see energy in the form of small flashes of light, sometimes circular and sometimes as irregular shapes of luminescence. Sometimes the flashes of light appear close to people, and oftentimes they hover around me. They're usually blue or purple, and at first they were easier to see against light surfaces like white sofas or white floors.

Years ago I began to show people how to see aura. Having developed the tools to do that, it appears that the Universe has now asked me to show people how to see other aspects of phenomena as well.

We each play a vital role in one another's journey. The amazing teachers in my life played an integral part in preparing me for the Rays—my Extra Celestial guides I originally met in a crop circle. Derek O'Neill is an Avatar and Ascended Master here to serve mankind as well as our threatened Mother Earth. His phenomenal ability to connect people to Source is transformational. Starr Fuentes is a library of esoteric knowledge as well as the lineage holder for the Mayan traditions of healing. Jodi Serota is a profound channel of the sound and vibration of Love. These are some of the individuals who have played a vital part in my unfolding. Their stories, as well as the Rays' and mine, are lovingly entwined in *Lineage*.

All of us in human bodies are students. Everyone who stands in front of us is our teacher. And while some of us in this Earth school appear to know more than others, they are simply here to assist the rest of us on our path. They remind us of who we are in truth, and it is through them that we can begin to truly access our power and learn to keep it for ourselves. There's no reason to give more power to our teachers—every one of us is a master and guru.

I met Dr. John Mack, the controversial Harvard psychiatrist, a few years ago. He did a fascinating study of "alien abductees" under hypnosis. I remember his line, "I didn't ask you to believe me; it's just true."

That is precisely what I will ask of *Lineage* readers. Much of what you read in these pages will challenge your views of reality and so much more. This information was given to me directly from the I Am Presence. Their love was the guiding force in writing this book, and now it is my offering of love to you.

When you can see what I see, you too will know what an amazing place the Universe is. Now is the time for all of us to access our own experience. The information included here is an opportunity for everyone to heal and explore our own personal relationship to the Divine. This is the time for each of us to choose that for ourselves, and when we do, we heal each other and our planet simultaneously.

BACKGROUND INFORMATION

ABOUT THE TEACHERS AND HEALERS IN
LINEAGE

Meryl Hershey Beck is an energy psychologist, healer, and teacher of many different healing modalities. She has periodically been Nancy Burson and her son Keir's traveling companion to vortexes in the British Isles since 2000. www.energizedforlife.com

John Burke is a physics researcher, inventor, and author, and part of the BLT Research Team, Inc. His knowledge of physics has assisted Nancy Burson in understanding and documenting the orbs and other phenomena in the United States and Europe.

Starr Fuentes is a Master teacher, healer, and lineage holder of the Mayan traditions. She teaches many different classes gleaned from her library of esoteric knowledge. www.starrfuentes.com

Bert Janssen is a Dutch documentary filmmaker and the producer/director of three films on crop circles. www.bertjanssen.com

Isabelle Kingston is a Master teacher, channel, and one of Britain's foremost psychics. She has dedicated her life to energizing and opening the land to receive the phenomena that became the crop circles.

Ti Mar is a psychic and remarkable channel for what Burson calls the Rays (or ECs) and what she has called the "Light World Visitors" for over 25 years. She speaks their language, conducts workshops, and has co-authored several books. www.timar.biz

Kyriacos Markides is an internationally recognized authority on esoteric Christianity. He is a sociology professor, author, and workshop facilitator from Cyprus who has written many books on Christian mysticism and healing.

Derek O'Neill is an Avatar and Ascended Master, as well as a psychotherapist, Swami, Master teacher, and healer. His lineage stems from the traditions of both Christ-consciousness and Hinduism, and his ability to connect people to Source is life-changing. www.bornfreenow.com, and www.creaconpremaagni.com

Rob Robb is a brilliant, intuitive life coach who travels constantly and is a beloved counselor for thousands. www.robrobb.com

MJ Sawyer is a vibrational sound specialist in healing brain chemistry disorders without medication. She has had great success in transforming depression, bipolar, OCD, ADD, ADHD, symptoms of autism, and anxiety disorders. www.mjsawyer.com

Jodi Serota is a vibrational healer, artist, and Master meta-physical educator. Her intuitive abilities and her remarkable sound healing skills are used to make major shifts in consciousness for individuals and groups at her multi-media events. www.jodiserota.com

Alan Steinfeld is the host of *New Realities TV*, which represents the leading edge of cable shows about consciousness. www.newrealities.com

Brook Still is a Master healer, teacher, and protégé of Derek O'Neill. Her intuition and gifts are held in the highest regard in the Burson household. www.creationcenter.org

Nancy Talbot is the president of BLT Research Team, Inc., and a foremost researcher and world authority on crop circles. www.bltresearch.com

Robbert van den Broeke is a Dutch medium and healer whose photographs of Light Beings are currently featured in books and on Dutch television. www.robbertvandenbroeke.com

CHAPTER ONE

ASK AND YOU SHALL RECEIVE

In early June 2005, I awoke to the presence of several tall, white beings asking my permission to insert some sort of device in the area between my shoulder blades. "Well, okay," I said. "If you're sure you guys know what you're doing." The device they implanted was a rectangular shape about eight inches long, six inches wide, and two inches high, with a flashing red light on one side. I remember thinking after I had given my permission that this really is okay, and it's not as if someone could x-ray me and find it. It's only light and it's in a different dimension. Every day for many years I had asked for better communication and the ability to clearly discern the messages from my own guidance. And slowly, it seemed, my wish had been granted. "Ask and you shall receive" is one of the basic laws of the Universe. I asked for the direct communication with my guides, and at last here we were, having a conversation.

That morning I woke with a very sore back, and I thought, "Well, of course my back is sore. That's a really big thing they put inside me." When I sat down to do my daily morning meditation, I distinctly heard two numbers, 18 and 75, and then "map coordinates." To prepare for an upcoming trip to Wiltshire, England, I'd put two maps of the area on the walls in my bedroom, one directly across from my bed and one to the right of it. Hearing the coordinates, I immediately looked at the maps of Wiltshire and discovered the map coordinates of 18/75 are at Smeathe's Ridge. Maybe a crop circle would fall there, or something else would happen. I had never heard of this place, but from the map I could see that it was quite near the home of my teacher, Isabelle Kingston, at Ogbourne St. George, near Marlborough.

The night that I put those maps up, I knew the balls of light would appear, as they had randomly during the past year. I had seen these brilliant white balls just a few times since my experience in the Sun and Moon crop circle a year earlier. They had appeared in a brilliant flash of light above my head at night, which had startled me. And now, they weren't hovering six feet in front of me, as they had one night in Wiltshire. They were right above me. As soon as I turned out the light, the brightest light appeared just over my head. Now I was definitely certain that what I had just seen was in the exact dimension we call reality. My heart pounded, and I found myself saying to them, "Okay, I know I said I'd have less fear if you were farther away, but it's still so startling because you're so bright and you came out of nowhere and then what happens to you? Are you still here?" And this wasn't my only level of fear, as it seemed I was experiencing fear on many levels. Was this really happening to me? Was there any other possible explanation? Was I hallucinating on a nightly basis?

In the days that followed, my body felt as if it were consistently trying to adjust to the device inside my back. My sensitive immune system made it suddenly harder to absorb food. I tried every method I could to adjust to the light communicator within me, but I didn't know how to adjust to what seemed to be my new role. It wasn't that I didn't want it, as I felt privileged to receive it. It was, I knew, part of the passage to my next assignment, all part of the journey. It didn't matter that it was a little difficult to breathe and that I felt like I was dragging myself about. I had wandered into my own version of *The Matrix* and had agreed to take the red pill instead of the blue. This was my choice.

I called my friend, Meryl Beck. We had traveled together many times over the years. Meryl revealed that she too felt something had been placed in her back. Our parallel experiences made sense to me. We were going to Wiltshire together very soon, and we'd be sharing a room as well. I suspected that her device and mine were connected to the balls of light I had first witnessed in Great Britain, which were now in my bedroom. After about ten days and a lot of phone conversations with teachers and friends, I decided it was time for my device to go.

As one of my dearest friends, I knew Jodi Serota's overall expertise would help. When I had first met her, I thought the sounds she made for healing were really strange. However, I've never doubted that Jodi is the real thing, a channel, and a true Master. I would watch her reaction when people asked her where the sounds she made came from. "From other dimensions," she'd tell them, as if that were an ordinary thing to say. "They came from the time before karmic patterning began," she'd continue. And in that moment, I knew from the reaction of the person asking the question whether or not he or she thought Jodi was a nut case or the real thing.

With Jodi in direct channel with the beings, I became fully aware that they were just waiting for me to ask them to remove the device. It ceased to be useful because it had already served its purpose many days before by completing the "download" of the information it contained. This experience was a continuance of my own personal lessons. Both God and the Universe would never ask me to do anything beyond my comfort level. I am always in charge. We each have choices for which the Universe, in return, responds. Real victimization is only possible if we ourselves allow it. Therefore, the placement of something within me gave me a way to look at some major issues for myself. There were plenty of boundary problems that rose to the surface from this experience. It was a reminder that I get to decide.

And in the bigger picture, over the years I've come to realize my purpose in this lifetime. In this round, I am to know and trust that I will survive unpunished for revealing what I know. In how many lifetimes had I been persecuted and killed? I don't know, nor is that important to know. This time I'll be allowed to be exactly who I am, with the freedom to deal with all the topics brought forth herein. Miracles aren't intended to make us comfortable. Miracles come through our own willingness to stretch and grow.

How was I to perceive my new reality? I began to remind myself of what I already knew. The most efficient way for the Universe to get our attention is by giving us what we fear the most.

For years I had carried judgment against anything related to UFOs,

Derek O'Neill, © 2006

forgetting that anything we're in resistance to is what we'll receive in abundance. Having taught at Harvard and worked with the FBI, I was convinced that in order to maintain my credibility, it wouldn't serve me to get involved with anything related to outer space and its inhabitants. Again, Dr. John Mack, the Harvard psychiatrist studying "abduction cases," served as a model. He had defended his tenure there in a court of law.

Yet I had to admit that I'd seen some angels, and obviously they could fly! How were some things possible and others not? My reality had been fraught with judgment and criticism. Clearly I was not the doer, and it wasn't up to me to decide what was and wasn't possible when, in fact, all things are possible.

I could just hear the Universe in response to my resistance. "Here's your assignment. If you can't stand the thought of people thinking you're too weird, look what we've got for you!"

As Derek O'Neill would say, "The Universe is hilarious!"

CHAPTER TWO

MIRACLE MEN

In 1997, Derek O'Neill was a psychotherapist and energy worker in Dublin, using a wide range of techniques with his clients, including his skills in hypnotherapy, healing, and psychic intuition. One day, he visited a bookstore with his wife Linda and daughter Orla. A book fell off the shelf onto his feet. He picked it up and saw that it was about an Indian Avatar called Sai Baba, who is worshipped by millions in India. The book's title is *Sai Baba, Man of Miracles*. At the same time, his daughter brought him a package of incense, and when Derek read the label, he saw it was "Sai Baba" incense. He asked the shopkeeper how much the book was, and the owner told him the shop had never carried that book. Nevertheless, he did sell it to Derek, as well as the incense, and they all left.

That night, Derek picked up the book and began reading. Then he put it aside, having decided it was "just crap." Later, however, he noticed the book had a glow to it. The next morning, all eight of Derek's patients called within the hour to cancel their appointments. Derek listened as one client after another phoned to say that something had unexpectedly come up. With the day suddenly free, he picked up the book again. And at the end of the day, Derek wrote a note that said, "My name is Derek. If you are who you say you are, send me Vibhuti, and I will come." Vibhuti is the sacred ash that is produced from the hands of the Indian or Hindi Masters, which is considered healing and holy. He addressed the envelope simply "Sai Baba, India," which is like sending something addressed to Paddy O'Brien to Ireland. Derek only told his wife and his colleague that he'd sent it and joked to Linda that "Now we'll all be going off to India to see God!" Then they forgot about it.

About three months later, Derek and his colleague were at The Mind, Health, and Body Exhibition in Dublin, where they were looking over the various products available. A stranger in an orange shirt tapped him on the shoulder and said, "Excuse me. Are you Derek O'Neill?"

Derek replied, "I am. Do I know you?"

The stranger said, "You know of me. May I speak to you?"

They sat down at a table, where the stranger proceeded to reveal the most intimate details of Derek's childhood. He said, "You were born with a mane of long black hair. You healed a child with whooping cough when you were five years old. It was your first experience in healing in this lifetime. When you were nine, your psychic awareness saved your mother's life when you didn't allow her to get on a bus that you knew would crash." Derek began to tremble, and a surge of energy rushed through him. The energy flooded his body as the stranger continued to tell him the details of his life. Derek was in a state of shock and fear as his body continued to tremble. At that point, the stranger passed Derek a small silver box and said, "You asked for Vibhuti; now you must come." He knew that this man must have been a messenger sent by Sai Baba, and at that same moment, Derek's colleague walked into a column upon realizing that Derek had just received a tin of Vibhuti from the stranger.

Derek and his colleague ran to a coffee shop nearby. Derek ordered coffee and was so rattled by the stranger that there wasn't much coffee left in the cup to drink. Then an Indian woman in a green sari appeared in the doorway of the coffee shop. She saw Derek and walked right up to him and said, "Haven't I just seen you talking with Sai Baba at the Mind, Health, and Body Exhibition?" Another surge of energy ran through him, and Derek trembled as waves of excitement and fear again flooded his entire body. Caught in the energy of her words, and startled by the rare sight of a woman in full Indian attire in Dublin, Derek had no idea who it really was that he had just seen at the Expo.

Two weeks later, Derek was on a plane to India. When he arrived at Puttaparthi, there were thousands of devotees waiting outside the ashram. Derek waded through the crowds of people, the poor and the hungry, and he was touched by the mass of humanity present there. He told someone in the crowd of perhaps 30,000 that Sai Baba had sent for him, and that he had come to see him. The man replied, "Yes, Sai Baba has sent for all of these people."

The overwhelming sight of all the sick, starving, and homeless children triggered memories of a different type of deprivation from Derek's own childhood. Why should a child be deprived of anything? These children had nothing. Derek was so moved that he made up his mind that "no child should live like this," and he understood his mission would be to somehow help these children.

Derek made his way to the accommodation office. As he walked in, the elderly man in charge screamed "Sai Ram, Sai Ram" at him very loudly. Startled at the intensity of his reprimand, somehow Derek understood that he'd forgotten to remove his shoes. He went out, removed his shoes, and came in again. The same man greeted him using the same words, only this time "Sai Ram" was used with incredible love and devotion. "So you're back!" Derek looked around, because the same man who had reprimanded him, this time spoke to him with a genuine outpouring of love. He had no idea what this ancient guy was talking about, because he'd never been there before. Derek said, "I'm sorry. You must be mistaken. I've never been here before." And then the ancient man said, "Derek, you have been here many times and in many lifetimes. Sai Baba has been waiting for you."

He led Derek to a very small room that accommodates twenty-one people. After dropping his things off, Derek went up to the roof to meditate, where he was met by a man who told him that he was to initiate him as a Karuna Reiki Master on that very roof the next day. According to Derek's friend, who was watching below, when the initiation took place, a rainstorm formed only over the roof of the ashram, accompanied by high winds and a rainbow over one side. Derek lost consciousness and didn't really remember anything. When he woke, he was alone. Later that day, Derek went to see the man who had initiated him to ask him a few questions about the notes he'd found in his pocket from his initiation on the roof.

When he went to visit the man's quarters, he was greeted by a Buddhist monk who asked if he was the Initiate. When Derek replied that he was, the monk bowed at his feet. Shocked at this gesture, the monk informed him that the man had left that morning. Sai Baba had told the man in a personal interview that he had to wait until the Initiate arrived before he could return home to his family. "How long did he wait?" Derek asked.

"Seven years," the monk answered.

At Derek's first Darshan, there were 20,000 people to see Sai Baba. He had an "Inner View" with Derek, in which Sai Baba transmitted everything Derek needed to know telepathically. Derek was to conduct workshops in America that would open people to their own truth, allowing them to love fully, and empowering them to become their own Masters. And the money he would make from his More Truth Will Set You Free workshops in America would be returned to India in the form of orphanages for needy children.

Prema Agni

Once Derek began to travel and teach workshops, he found himself caught between his commitment to his wife and children and his service to God. He wanted and needed the freedom to expand, and he was also aware that he was pulling away to do that. He knew he was hurting them all because he was not present for them, adding more anger and frustration to what the family was feeling. Psychologically, Linda became the angry, controlling mother who beat and abused him, and Derek was mirroring to Linda the father who had died and "abandoned" her as a child. Even as qualified psychotherapists with their issues completely out in the open, the emotional feelings remained. They both agreed it was an uncomfortable place they were at in that moment. If it was meant to work out, it would. On that, they both agreed.

I first met Derek and Linda O'Neill in the coffee shop downstairs from the New Life Expo in October of 2002. Keir and I had just returned from our first trip to Ireland (with Isabelle and Meryl) and I was pleased to meet an Irishman on this side of the Atlantic. He said,

"My guides instructed me to give you this. It's my last flier." I was taken with his mischievous smile, his Irish charm, and his reference to Merlin energies in his flier. I immediately invited him to my party the following night. He said he had just met Starr Fuentes, and she had also invited him. He thanked me, but he and Linda were leaving the next day. Starr told me later that she had spotted Derek's aura from way across the room.

Derek O'Neill, © 2006

I attended one of Derek's More Truth Will Set You Free workshops in June 2003. It was profound. Up until that point, I had mostly relied on places—high-energy vortexes—to serve as vehicles to connect me with Source. Being in Derek's presence, I experienced a similar high-energy connection to Source, in that the places he could take me were just as sacred. It was obvious that he could hold massive amounts of energy for thousands of people at a time. Derek fills the room with so much loving energy that it allows individuals the ability to accelerate their spiritual growth. His unique use of music accompanies great flows of energy that permeate all levels of the body.

Attending one of his workshops is a rare opportunity to completely open and explore the depths of who we are. He taught us how to make the Prema Agni symbol, which stands for the fire of Divine Love. It's the symbol he's been instructed to bring to the world that will open the flow of love in every heart. It's very difficult to describe his workshops, but I always take notes.

"You know they're beginning to call me the spiritual DJ," Derek said, "and do you know why? I use music and meditation to allow you

Aura photo of the Prema Agni, © 2006, in collaboration with Dr. Konstantin Korotkov

to open your own truth and bring you closer to God. And when I say God, you can just plug in any word that your heart connects to—whatever name that is. Out of the six billion people on the planet, fifty percent are comfortable using that word. And another forty-five percent call that energy something else. Buddha, Allah, whatever a person most aligns with is the name to use." After a pause, he went on, "And I want to thank all of you here today, because the $150 that you gave us to be here will feed and house one child in India for a whole year." Everyone in the audience responded by clapping. He continued, "And India is just the starting point. Every child must be fed, housed, educated, and loved. Right now. I see such a good example of what God shows me that is so wonderful. This man here, can I ask you, do you have a pain periodically in the back of your neck?" The man in question responded affirmatively. Derek asked, "And you carry a mark there as well?"

"Yes," responded the man.

"This is where the arrow that killed him in his last lifetime entered his body, just there," Derek proclaimed. "I'm not asking you to believe in reincarnation. It's just true!"

"And the young man with the red hair. Do you know you were with 'JC' and his buddies in his lifetime?" The red-haired man nodded his head, indicating he did. "And did you know what your purpose was in that lifetime?" The young man nodded his head yes. "Do you know your purpose in this lifetime?" Yes, he indicated again. "Do you know you carry a mark from that lifetime that should be about here?" and Derek pointed to a spot on the inside of his left arm, just above his elbow. The young man lifted his shirt to reveal a plum-sized mark that Derek said was where they'd begun beating him to death. It was finally a new piece of information that he hadn't known before.

Then Derek asked the audience, "How many of you would agree with these two statements? God creates everything." A show of hands went up.

"We create our own reality." More hands went up. "In fact, both are true," Derek said.

"We absolutely create our own reality, AND we are not the doer. Everything is Divine Will. The only way to live is to open your heart. And the more we live in our hearts in truth and integrity, the more we become our own scriptwriters. And understand the script is only written one line ahead.

"Everything that we're getting is guidance. Everything is a message. Watch and listen. All the answers lie within us.

"Okay, now this piece of music is going to connect you to the Angelic realms and your own Divine guidance, so I want you to close your eyes and keep them closed. Now, if you hear the person next to you sniffling (and he showed us an example of someone sniffling), don't comfort them. If you feel the person next to you doing this (he showed us someone crying and shaking), don't touch them." He paused. "And if you see someone going like this (shaking and crying violently), don't help them. Leave them alone, because they're with God. Let's all remember now that emotions are energy in motion. Feel the emotion and know that you are God. And don't give your power to me or anyone else. You be your own guru and Master. And there's no need to give Jesus or Allah or Buddha or whoever you honor more power. They have enough of their own.

"Because the more we understand that God is standing in front of us always, whether we're looking into a mirror or standing in front of our mates or children, each of us is a part of God. The only sin that man carries is his belief that we are separate from God. We will be tested many ways so we can prove to ourselves that we're right. All our words can be summed up in these three letters: E G O. These letters are the difference between the Masters and humanity."

What Does Love Look Like?

After I returned from Derek's weeklong workshop in Ireland, I was shown an image of what I can only describe as two beings making love. These luminescent white beings looked solid enough to be more than light. With love and complete joy, they hugged and embraced each other. I have no idea who or what they were. I was just glad they were so happy together. Perhaps they were shown to me as a way for me to understand that there are a multitude of ways to love within the Universe—look how diverse it is!

About the time that Mother Mary began dancing, I was shown an image of another face—what I can only describe as an "alien" face. I'm not proud to say that my first reaction was, frankly—eew! All the training in taking pictures of craniofacial kids, all those cancer survivors I'd met and then photographed that I'd seen with their facial prosthetics off, and my reaction was eew! And then being totally embarrassed, I said, "Well, you guys kind of look like you have insect faces, and they're okay, those insect faces. I just have to get used to them."

CHAPTER THREE

THREE ASPECTS OF PERCEPTION

In 1968, after two years studying at Colorado Women's College, I quit and moved to New York City to be an artist. I intended to transfer to NYU, but ended up freelancing mechanicals for *The New York Times* instead. That was my day job on and off for fifteen years, and I made my art at night.

I decided that I wanted my art to deal with three different aspects of perception: how we perceive ourselves; how we perceive each other; and how we perceive ourselves within the Universe. I didn't know how I would accomplish these through my art, nor did I have any idea how guided my path would be in exploring these issues. I didn't realize that these interests were to be catalysts for my soul's journey in this lifetime.

When I first arrived in New York, I visited a show called *The Machine as Seen at the End of the Mechanical Age* at the Museum of Modern Art. I loved that the show was participatory and that people were enjoying interacting with the art. It was on one of my first nights in my studio apartment in Greenwich Village that I began to formulate the idea to create an interactive machine that would allow people to see how they would age. I met a painter who was showing her work on the street in the Village, and she told me about an organization called EAT, Experiments in Art and Technology. EAT was renowned artist Robert Rauschenberg's organization, where artists and scientists were paired together. I contacted the people at EAT and met with a scientist they recommended to discuss my idea. EAT introduced me to Carl Machover, a computer graphic consultant who was working with state-of-the-art computers in White Plains, New York. But state-of-the-art in 1968 wasn't impressive. There was a pad-and-pen system to draw with, and that was all. I was not enthusiastic and asked, "How will this help me age people?" He replied, "It can't. You'll have to wait for the technology to catch up."

In 1976, eight years later, Carl advised me to contact MIT, and I started looking into advances in computer graphic technology. After an initial conversation with Nicholas Negroponte, the head of the department at MIT now called the Media Lab, I was invited to develop my idea there. Nicholas said, "Oh, yeah, we can do that. We can probably even do that in color."

It was a good example of how well the Universe can set us on our path. I was at MIT at just the right moment, and my aging project became one of the first times the human face was digitized and manipulated. It was a very slow process, taking several minutes to scan a face. Our models lay on the floor with the camera mounted above them, and we told them when they could blink.

I left MIT with videotape that showed three faces aging. Two stills from that tape were released to one of the wire services, and they were published worldwide. The response was enormous. Reporters from the *National Enquirer* were looking around MIT for a black box that aged people. MIT's administrative office called me and asked who I was and where was this black box. I said, "There is no black box. There's just a videotape of three people aging."

Thomas Schneider, a student there at the time, and I got a patent in 1981 on what we referred to at the time as "warping." And that, in essence, became the basis of what is now called morphing. I met Richard Carling, who was working around the corner from MIT at Computer Corporation of America. Richard, his friend and colleague David Kramlich, and I would work on the composites on weekends. The process was very time-consuming, as it took twenty-five minutes to warp each face. Our first commission was for *People* magazine, who asked us to age some celebrities, including Princess Diana, John Travolta, Brooke Shields, and JFK, Jr. Eventually, David Kramlich and I expanded the aging process to include the updating of missing children as well as adults, and the FBI and National Center for Missing Children obtained our software. We were featured on national television, along with the updates of the children who were missing. Those shows enabled us to find at least four children in the first year alone.

While working with families of missing children, I realized that intuitively I could feel whether the child was dead or alive, and sometimes I could sense what had happened to that child as soon as his or her image popped up on the screen.

Years later I ended up teaching at NYU and Harvard. It felt surreal. I was thrilled to be asked to teach at the college level, especially after never earning a degree myself. The commute to Harvard felt like visiting a foreign country each week. How ironic, though, that I had moved to New York City expecting to finish college by going to NYU. Instead, I ended up teaching there in the photography department. Many years later, the Grey Art Gallery, NYU's museum, was home to my twenty-five year retrospective exhibition.

What Does Normal Look Like?

I didn't understand why I've never really felt that I'm a photographer until the past few years. It's the Universe that is the artist, photographer, inventor, healer, writer, and everything that we are. I am not the doer. God/Spirit/the Universe is that. I am the channel, instrument, and collaborator, as I believe we all are, for Source to flow through us. I don't pray to be a better artist or writer, I ask to be a clearer channel for Source to come through me. When we are open to receive, everything is a message. The key is the consciousness to keep following those messages.

As I watch the swirling blue masses above me each night in my bedroom, I have become aware that the black holes I sometimes see within them are eyes. Have my experiences as a photographer prepared me to see them? Knowing that it's easier for me to see them in a form that I find less unsettling, they choose to interact with me from my reference/preference point. They're right about this. It is still hard for me to view them in that form. It's such an implant that I have from so many decades of anti-alien propaganda that I still carry this visual judgment—this prejudice—which I'm frankly not comfortable with at this time.

When will my human judgments end? If someone like me who works daily on my conscious awareness is so prone to judgment of appearance, I can clearly understand how most humans may be slow to catch up. Have I not become something of an expert on faces, both "normal" and "abnormal"?

In 1991, I began to photograph children with craniofacial disorders and adults with facial deformities caused by cancer. The series echoed my own facial trauma I had developed from a surgery for a wisdom tooth that hadn't healed well. I had manifested a hole in the bone, causing pain in my jaw and eventual facial atrophy that left me with daily pain for several years. There was no better way to provide an example for myself of how we create our own reality than manifesting my own deformity to align with the subjects in my photographs. I had literally taken on their pain, and I began to really see the connection between the mind and the body in a new way.

I met Isaiah Buggs through a doctor friend of mine at Sloan Kettering. My friend was a surgeon there who fit patients who had facial cancers with prosthetics to cover the holes from their surgeries. I did rounds with him a few times, and he left me alone with Mr. Buggs while he went to fix his prosthesis. With his device removed, I could see the inside of his skull. I didn't even realize that it was possible for anyone to live with that much empty space carved out of the head. I could have gotten my entire hand in there.

Mr. Buggs was a very kind man, and we talked and laughed for the next half hour until my doctor friend returned with his prosthesis fixed. I didn't think the doctor really had to leave me with Mr. Buggs for so long. It was his way of testing me to see if I'd be able to handle his appearance and stay in my heart. A few months later, I took some beautiful large Polaroids of Mr. Buggs, posing with pride in his majesty, a Master of self-acceptance. Now it seems as if he was only my first round of tests from the Universe.

Six years of experience with deformity, the invention of facial morphing, and *Star Wars* didn't fully prepare me to see the beings that share my home. According to studies, it only takes us three to five seconds to judge someone based solely on their appearance. Yet, if we can focus a little longer, taking time for the heart to intervene in the brain-to-eye connection, we can shift our judgments. It's been described as the longest journey in the world, the one from the head to the heart. Are we, as humans, capable of doing that now? Am I? No matter what the being in front of us looks like, can we love them without judgment?

CHAPTER FOUR

SEEING AND BELIEVING

It was through Jodi Serota's presence in my life that I learned to focus and fine-tune my intentions. In fact, it was she who taught me how to pray more effectively. A pivotal figure in my life, she is a mixture of steadfast grounded-ness and angelic poise. With five hundred people who attended her Harmonic Concordance Concert on November 8, 2003, our mutual friend MJ Sawyer and I sat like proud parents in the audience, knowing that someday, thousands would come to hear her sounds and music.

I got to know Jodi on a trip to Casa Alma to celebrate the sixtieth birthday of Starr Fuentes, whom I had recently photographed.

Jodi was sleeping in the smaller room adjacent to the "dorm" room I was in, and she'd spent most of the first night there writing pages of numerical code she was receiving from the UFO that had parked itself right outside her window. I thought she was pretty "out there"—and now she teases me that I am too. I still remind her that at least in part, it all began through her!

In the summer of 2000, I'd gone to spend the night at Jodi's house, specifically to see the "beings" that I'd heard her say appeared on her lawn in response to her sounds, the tones and vibrational languages she'd channeled for many years. She was at once so odd, yet so reassuringly normal! Over the years, she'd healed my body often with the sounds that came through her. And her sense of humor serves as a continual delight. I have at least as much gratitude for that characteristic as her otherworldly abilities.

That first night at her house, when it was as dark as it could get, we took flashlights and proceeded out to the clearing of Jodi's lawn, holding hands. Jodi channeled the necessary sounds that immediately formed a white haze in the darkness around us. We could only make out heads and shoulders of the white beings that encircled us, and we each felt their energy palpably. It was an extraordinary moment, and through our brief dialogue with them, all seemed well in the world. I remember vividly the streaks of red light I'd seen, which were so big they seemed like some sort of vehicle they'd arrived on. It was an experience I was reluctant to discuss with anyone, but I had made drawings of both the beings and the red streaks of light I had seen in the sky.

Seeing and Believing became the title of my retrospective in the year 2002. It might have been called "Seeing is Believing," but by 2002, it was my belief that sometimes God and the Universe require that we believe before we can see. I knew clearly then that all souls didn't come from the Earth.

CHAPTER FIVE

WHY DOES SHE DANCE?

The device, or light-communicator, was removed the night Jodi channeled the beings for me. I was mostly asleep at the time, but awake enough to feel my body vibrating in a way that I had never before experienced. Those odd vibrations sent waves of gratitude through me for all the closeness I have with my earthling teachers who lovingly guide me with their experience in these matters. A few nights later, Jodi stopped by to get a feel for my bedroom, which had suddenly become an increasingly active vortex. When I turned out the light, Jodi focused on my glow-in-the-dark Mary, a two-inch plastic Madonna I had purchased in Santa Monica in 2004. Mary fades when the light goes out and her feminine presence is soothing to me when I fall asleep at night.

Jodi and I often laugh because our mothers were both named Lois. As we sat in the darkness, my mother Lois, who passed away years ago, appeared beside me, credibly announcing herself by the name "Funny Face" she had unfortunately been called by her parents. As a child growing up Reform Jewish in the Midwest, I have only in recent years come to consider Mother Mary as a symbol of the Divine Feminine. Over the years, my faith grew into an eclectic blend of Western belief systems. My father was gentile and my mother Jewish, so in the eyes of other Jews, I was considered a Jew. Yet my mother grew up in a

Catholic neighborhood. I was probably the only kid in the Midwest whose Jewish mom gave her a crucifix. I liked it because it had a tiny peephole in the center, and when you put your eye up to it, you could see the Lord's Prayer printed inside. I would pray holding onto that.

In 2004, I combined Mary's image with that of Isis and Quan Yin to create the *Goddess*, the mate for my *One* image I had reworked the year before (Jesus, Mohammed, Buddha). In 2000, I created a piece called *The Guys Who Look Like Jesus.* I ran some ads seeking men of all ethnicities who resembled Jesus. It was my exploration into the specific motivation behind their choice to resemble Jesus. It was also my way of challenging accepted notions of what Jesus looked like. Ultimately, the men I chose were all different races, the antithesis of most art historical depictions of Jesus.

I also photographed women who resemble Madonnas for the series, *The Women Who Look like Mary.* For me, Mary represents the Divine Feminine appearing in all women. Again, my motivation behind this new series of images is to investigate the energy of the Divine Mother within each of us as represented by each of these women. And this, too, was my way of challenging accepted notions of the ethnicity of the Divine Mother, as I chose a variety of women representing ethnic diversity.

That night, though, Jodi noticed that glow-in-the-dark Mary was, well, moving. In fact, it looked like she was dancing. We sat in bed and watched her dancing, twirling, moving back and forth across what seemed about a foot in length along the edge of the TV monitor (that's never used as a TV, but rather for watching tapes shot in the European PAL system) across from my bed. Jodi commented that it looked like animation, and I agreed. Mary's movement was bizarre and eerie, I first thought. I found myself afraid that she might fall off the edge as she moved from one side to the other. We could even see her legs and arms, which was odd, because Mary's traditional outfit kind of hides her legs and arms. Yet how could she be dancing? Her movements were amazing, but what were we watching? How was all this happening, and, more important, were we watching a miracle?

In November of 2004, there were over a million hits on eBay relating to the sale of a Marian apparition on a toasted cheese sandwich. Clearly we are hungry for miracles. The number of Mary apparitions are increasing these days, in keeping with the historical lineage of appearances by the Holy Mother that have proliferated since A.D. 40, when she was still alive. Millions flock to places like Lourdes, Fatima, and Medjugorje annually. Locally, even Bayside, Queens, has been the site of Mary revelations in recent years. Marian images have been said to produce miracle cures, prophecies, apocalyptic warnings, and conversions from agnosticism. Presently, record numbers of Mary statues appear to weep an array of fluids, including tears, oils, perfumes, and blood. Previous to Marian devotion, the ancients worshipped the mother goddess of divine feminine energies, represented by Athena or Isis. Could my little Mary statue be considered theophany, a manifestation of God?

Mary's movements sent waves of anxiety through me, as I didn't know what to expect when Jodi left. This was so utterly weird. What would I do if Mary fell off the monitor? Would I pick her up? Or would I be too frozen to my bed to move? I would have welcomed the dawn at that moment, but it was only just midnight. I was relieved that Mary's show continued after Jodi left, even though I found this new phenomenon intimidating. I had grown accustomed to using Jodi's ability to channel, to come to my rescue instead of relying more on my own ability to communicate with Source. And for the past two years, Jodi had accompanied me on my adventures in Wiltshire. Her ability to bring in sound through the realms had manifested the first beings I had ever seen on her lawn some years earlier. Clearly, Mary is running on some sort of energy. But whose energy is it?

CHAPTER SIX

FROM BIRTH TO BIRTH

I met Kyriacos Markides, the sociologist-turned-mystic, in 1987, when I signed up for his workshop at The Open Center, a spiritual learning center around the corner from where I live. Kyriacos is a grounded and sensible social scientist whose wide smile is always reassuring. He teaches with grace and ease. He published several books in the 1980s about a healer called Daskalos, a fellow Cypriot whose healings were well-documented and whose reputation was well-known throughout the Middle East, Greece, and Cyprus. We became friends, and eventually he and his wife accepted my invitation to stay with me, and they did whenever he taught a workshop.

Listening to Kyriacos talk about Daskalos and his circle of healers called the Erevna circle in Cyprus was my introduction to energy healing, which had in previous decades been referred to as the "laying on of hands." Most currently, much of what is called energy healing is labeled under "Reiki," a form of healing that is commonly taught throughout the U.S. These days, Reiki practitioners are so common-place and well accepted that Children's Hospital in Boston has them on staff for pain management after children's surgeries.

David Kramlich (my partner in facial morphing and my "spousal equivalent" since 1980) and I had finally moved in together. We wanted to have a child, our very own composite. We'd gotten married in 1987, and since I was thirty-nine at the time, we started trying to conceive right away. As month after month went by with no pregnancy, I called Kyriacos to ask for the Erevna circle's help in conceiving a child.

I had been wearing the Erevna symbol around my neck since Kyriacos gave me one as a gift when he had come to stay one weekend. It is actually three symbols combined. The outside symbol is a circle, which represents the oneness of all there is, or God. The middle symbol consists of two triangles. The downward triangle symbolizes God descending to man, and the upward triangle, man ascending to God. Together they form the Star of David (or Jewish Star), also referred to as the Seal of Solomon, the six-pointed star. The inside symbol is the Christian cross, representing the four elements (earth, air, fire, water) of early Christian thought. It remains on my altar because it represents what I refer to as oneness, or the unity of all religions through love.

The Erevna group and Daskalos as its leader sent prayers for me to conceive, and in July 1988, I did. My son Keir was born in early March 1989. I began to feel a presence around me a month or so before his conception, and I later recognized that energy as his.

From the beginning of our baby name search, Keir was the only name that resonated with both David and me. It was the actor, Keir Dullea, who was the sole survivor of the computer in Stanley Kubrick's film, *2001: A Space Odyssey*, who served as inspiration. And even though I was aware that Keir is Gaelic for small and dark-skinned, which I knew wouldn't describe him, the name still felt like a fit. Years later, my teacher Isabelle Kingston handed Keir a postcard she'd found with information about his name. The most famous Kieran (Keir is a derivative) was Seir Kieran, the first Saint of Ireland, who founded the Saighir monastery—and the Saint's day for St. Kieran (or spelled St. Ciaran) is March 5, my son's exact birthday.

I spent months preparing myself to give birth and doing all the self-hypnosis, meditation, and visualization I had used as tools for years. I intended that labor be brief, and it only took a total of seven hours. Seven-pound-eleven-ounce Keir was born a week early. I weighed a hundred and one pounds before my pregnancy, and baby Keir got too big for me to push out on my own, so forceps were used to pull him out. My bladder shut down, and my tailbone fractured while giving birth. Two days later, I developed an infection with high fever, and because of the high fever I wasn't permitted to hold or nurse my new-born son. When David took Keir home, the separation from my healthy baby converged with guilt over leaving him temporarily moth-erless. Engulfed in fear, I struggled with the IVs of different antibiotics and nightly spikes of fever for a week. This trauma felt like a memory of dying in childbirth, an implant from a former time that I couldn't shake.

In the midst of the many infections that followed over the next sev-eral years, there were too many rounds of IVs of antibiotics for my immune system to withstand, and I developed mal-absorption.

Had it started with Keir's birth? No. In fact, it had started before mine. I consider labels disempowering, but for the sake of clarity, I will say that I am what is called a DES Daughter. When my mother was pregnant with me, she was given a drug called Diethelstylbestrol, the first artificially produced hormone. It was manufactured and promot-ed by all the big drug companies in the late 1940s and on through part of the 1960s, even though the manufacturers knew there was direct evidence linking the drug to certain forms of cancer. Decades later, group lawsuits were settled with large payments from the drug compa-nies. Studies of DES daughters have found them to be more prone to everything from vaginal cancer to every kind of immune disorder to infertility. I felt lucky to have had a child. After having had some DES-related problems in my twenties, I had chosen to put it all behind me, not fully recognizing the additional risks of giving birth at age forty-one.

Many times during Keir's first years, I wondered if perhaps subcon-sciously I hadn't really wanted a child at all. "Look how sick I am" became the constant chatter inside my head, accompanied by "how is it possible to get well again?" My body reflected that, and with the mal-absorption, my weight dropped to 80 pounds. Indeed, my message had become "I am not enough." I was disappearing.

Over the years, I learned to honor the part of me that wasn't certain about being a parent. I felt guilty for feeling that I had lost my health to become a parent, and I felt guilty for wanting to be healthy again. I was a victim of my guilt. I loved my son, but hated not having the energy to keep up with him, to be the good mother and the perfect nurturer.

The physical body is always a reflection of the "dis-ease" within. It wasn't that I was such a terrible mother. I was just a mother with a stomach ache, low-grade fever, and very little energy. I enjoyed being with Keir, but was distracted and impatient at my worst. My body was in pain, and the pain was a mirror of my fear. I was losing my marriage as I watched my husband draw farther into himself and away from "us." I didn't love myself, and he didn't love me either. It was all a reflection. We were, as relationships are, the perfect mirror for each other.

A medical diagnosis in 1996 finally found the reason for my mal-absorption. There is a form of Candida that lives in the lining of the stomach, called Candida Glabrada. It is rarely seen, and then mostly in cases of end-stage cancer, or AIDS patients. Because of overdoses of broad-spectrum antibiotics, more cases of Glabrada are appearing that aren't treatable by the medical profession. I was told from the time it was diagnosed, there was no way to get rid of the organism complete-ly, as it's capable of burying deep within the stomach lining for months with or without food. So the question was, "How do I get well?" The answer seemed to be to "finesse it," and, over time, we would cohabit peacefully.

Then I met a Russian healer who is the only one I have ever seen work directly through the bone marrow, heating the blood stream and actually raising the energy of the immune system. I met him in the late 1990s, and with his direction, I learned how to use his techniques on myself as well as others. Once I began specifically to address my immune system by working on my own body on a daily basis, I devel-oped my own tools for improving my health. And as my own energy to heal myself strengthened, my frequency increased. With that amount of energy flowing through me, I was able to adjust my own immune system simply by "being."

CHAPTER SEVEN

MY HUMAN LINEAGE

Rob Robb is a brilliant intuitive life coach who travels and teaches around the country. From the first conversation we had, his intuition about Keir empowered me to parent him from a slightly different point of view.

He's an Indigo child, Rob told me, not that I've ever wanted to place a label on him. He has a dark bluish-purple aura around him, the aura color characteristic of those with an expanded sense of awareness, who are here to assist in healing our planet. Knowing this, I knew I had just been handed the key to parenting Keir. Through Rob, I understood there wasn't anything Keir didn't know about God and the Universe, so my son would in essence be my teacher. Of course, our children are always our teachers, and Keir more than most.

Keir arrived with an innate understanding of God and the Universe that was apparent from a very early age. He somehow just "got it all." It was just the way he came into this life, and he recognized that about himself as well.

I remember that Keir knew from a very early age that his soul had explored other options before he chose David and me as parents. He'd told me about a really nice couple in Minnesota, and the man sold cars. But Keir decided that it was just too cold up there. Another candidate was a teacher and his wife in Kansas. They were great, but they were going to have a lot of other kids, and he wanted all the attention.

I began to recognize that Keir wasn't an ordinary "normal" child— and no other child is, either. There was no way to define "normal." In fact "Normal" is really just a town in Illinois. When Keir was almost two years old, I heard about a book called *How to Talk so Kids Will Listen and Listen so Kids Will Talk* by Adele Faber and Elaine Mazlish, first published in 1980 by Avon Books. The *How to Talk* book provided real tools to communicate that transformed our relationship. I remember in the middle of my giving him a bath when he was two, he said "Mommy, you're using such good words with me." It was a validation and a new empowering beginning to my relationship with my child. Each new stage of development, as well as each new day, became a vehicle to understand the effect of my words on this extraordinary child. Good mothers aren't born to it; they are created out of the conscious understanding of who they are themselves.

Remember the Light

When Keir was seven I met Nancy Johnson, my first healer. It was from my relationship with her that I began to explore the mind/body connection and allow that I was at least in part responsible for my disease. I came to understand that illness is always a journey.

And even though I'd had this idea of capturing energy on regular film years before, Nancy was the first healer I photographed. I had asked Kyriacos about going to Cyprus to photograph Daskalos before Keir was born, but he had not been interested.

Even though I was sick and needed healing, it seemed that I also arrived at Nancy's for another purpose. I wanted to prove the effectiveness of energy healing by providing evidence of the existence of energy through my images. There was no disputing the fact that the effects on the images I'd taken of Nancy couldn't be explained in my mind as anything other than energy. One-and-one-third frames on the contact sheet showed a green haze around her. The rest of the images on the contact sheet were all white. Since Nancy used color to heal, it seemed especially significant that my camera had actually caught her exact specialty on film. So I came to regard this image as the first real evidence that it's possible to capture energy with a regular camera.

Nancy's Saturday afternoon meditations played a major role in my spiritual growth and introduced me to others who would change my life as well. During one of our group walks downtown, Kevin Dowling turned to me and said, "You know, you might want to think about strengthening your relationship to God." That was a helpful tip and one of those transformational moments. And then I met Russell Burke, who introduced me to boogie-busting (ridding oneself of energies that no longer serve us), and Russell taught a whole group of us Access, Gary Douglas's set of tools for consciousness.

Nancy's healing space opened all the doorways to all the pathways that lay ahead. Healing was in the air. I began to share my new knowledge with Keir, and, at the age of seven, he began healing his classmates. It was as natural to him as breathing. Keir described how he would send energy to a child or a teacher who had a stomachache or headache. Many of the healers I photographed had become my friends, so there were lots of healers around the house. It all seemed so perfectly orchestrated. After all, Keir's conception had been prayed for by Daskalos and the Erevna group in Cyprus, and Daskalos had been one of the most powerful healers on the planet until his death in 1995.

Our knowledge of energy became the best new toy for Keir and me. Together, we would make balls of energy with our hands as we rode in taxis and then toss them out the window to people on the street. It was our gift from the Universe. So many years before I had wondered what lies between us . . . between all of us. It seemed part of my soul's journey to create art about how we perceive ourselves within the universe. And I had finally been given the answer. What connects us all is simply energy.

When I brought my Harvard students to New York one weekend, I mentioned Nancy Johnson's Saturday meditation to them as something recommended, but not required. To my surprise, they all showed up. And in the weeks that followed, almost every one of them confided to me the amazing experience that they had had while there that day. It was remarkable proof of the power of that room to transform all who entered.

There was a tremendous blue presence that we referred to as my blue angel that would come and rest on my shoulders and heal me during the meditation each week. There were times this huge presence was so palpable that I could barely breathe. Nancy would smile at the consistency of this blue angelic presence each week, and she would describe to me what I felt but couldn't see. All of this and so much more came from that brilliant, sacred vortex on Tenth Street that was Nancy's transcendent healing space. Her heart embraced and cradled us on our journeys each week, and her steadfast grounded-ness guided our collective and personal flights.

When my first book of writing (there are four books of photography that preceded it), *Focus*, came out in 2004, I was thrilled to hear Nancy's voice on the phone praising my book and was honored when she recommended it to others. Her gifts and her vision were magnificent, and she saw into people's bodies with profound integrity. What a privilege it was that my first experience with a healer was with Nancy. She had the ability to put a stone on your head and guide you anywhere you wanted to go. It was she who took me on a journey so profound that I'd like to recall it here.

I had come to see Nancy (1996) because of health issues I couldn't resolve, and I'd been around the medical block with no real answers. Nancy felt the drug my mother had taken when she was pregnant with me seemed to be the place to start, and she told me that, unless I saw my first home, there would be no place that would ever feel safe. I remember her hands around my head and a stone on my forehead, and suddenly I found myself back in my mother's womb. Then without warning, it was as if a black curtain came down around me, my stomach got queasy, and I realized that this is what happened to my body every time my mother had taken that drug. It was terrifying. I shook and cried and gripped Nancy's arm though my sobs. And Nancy said, with masterful reassurance, "I promise you that you will never in your life be more frightened than you are at this moment." She sent in the Angels for protection, and that was the first time I actually saw anything so clearly in another dimension. I was brand new at this "expanded vision stuff."

It was the fluttering of luminescent angel wings that brought the greatest reassurance. And when I think back on that journey, I realize that the gift Nancy passed on to me that day was the courage to be myself. If there would never be anything that scary in my life again, I had truly been handed the key to my own empowerment. She'd helped me transcend my fears, and it felt as if she removed fear as an option in my life.

When Nancy Johnson died in 2005, I came back to her space once more. I spotted the little blue angel that I made for her one Christmas, still right where she placed it years before. With her sisters gathered around in the space where it all began, we meditated, and I saw Nancy standing in the middle of the circle, a bit above us. She said, "Remember the Light." Then, as if for confirmation, she folded her hands together. It was a quintessential Nancy gesture that I hadn't seen in many years. It was as if she were saying yes, it's really me up here, and how great that you're aware that I'm right here, just on the other side. Her closest friends borrowed the large photo of Nancy with the green glow for her memorial service. As hundreds of us stared up at her photo that had been placed on the church altar, we watched the green glow in the photo shift and change before our eyes.

Indigo Life

Keir developed a game with his dad called "Guess what car it is." Whenever they were on the street together, they would each point to a car and try to guess the make. Keir would always win this one, because he could hear the answers provided to him by his guidance system. Specifically, his guide Merlin was always there for him. ("Merlin" is a form of energy appearing as the collective consciousness of wisdom, magic, and transformation, and for me is often represented by the appearance of purple light.) It even seemed odd to Keir that Merlin would know the manufacturers of such contemporary vehicles, but Ascended Masters know everything. It didn't matter how obscure the model, Keir was going to have the right answer, because the answers weren't coming from him. Keir also used this system to get the answers on his tests during his first years at school. Although at some point early on, he stopped, switching off his guidance to access the information he needed on his own.

Rob Robb, by then our trusted friend, had told Keir how he used to drive his math teachers crazy when he would tell them angel A, B, or C had given him the answer. Not only was he always right, there was no possible way to work those math problems out as fast as Rob would know the answers without some sort of Divine Guidance.

One night when Keir was nine I slept on the floor of his room, because there were fumes of some sort on my side of the loft. All night long, I heard different kinds of sounds that I realized were doorbells going off in different dimensions. The next morning, I asked Keir who was visiting him at night. He said, "Well, you know, I really like to hear their stories. And I told you, it's hard for me to go to sleep sometimes."

"Yes," I said, "but you didn't tell me why it was hard for you to sleep! How many are coming at night?" I asked him.

"Depends on the night," we answered simultaneously.

"You know, Keir," I said, "You might want to edit who comes to you. I mean, you wouldn't want to let just anyone in your room, would you?" And then I added, "And you do mention that they could choose to go into Light, right?"

"Yeah, yeah," he answered. "That's why they're there. I've started getting rid of a few I've seen in the subway sometimes, too. They kind of smell bad and they're way too dumb to find their way out." He paused.

"What is it?" I asked.

"I've seen a few presidents lately."

"How do you know they're presidents? Are they talking to you?" I asked.

"No, they're not saying anything, but they look just like some of the guys in that president's book."

"Are you interested in politics, Keir?" I asked him.

"No," he said.

"Thank God," I said. "Send them away!"

I struggled with my health through Keir's first years while at the same time David and I worked hard to learn how to communicate with each other. The thin, unhealthy me wasn't the one he had chosen. The support that I needed to feel nourished and nurtured had not been forthcoming, and my reaction to his reaction felt like an angry threat. Keir sensed the distance between his parents, and, on many occasions, he would place our hands together in the apparent hope that they would never come apart. But that was not our destiny, and David left in 1998 when Keir was nine.

David moved into another loft directly upstairs from us. Before he left, I asked him to promise that he would never ask our child to choose between his father and his God. He has always honored this agreement.

One morning I got a call from both of them. David said, "I think that from what Keir's describing he's seeing energy on the ceiling." Then Keir got on the phone. He said, "There's all this light coming from Dad's skylight, and it's covering everything. It's white, and it's really bright."

"Is it around people?" I asked him.

"It's around Dad."

I told him, "Go look in a mirror and see if it's around you."

"Yes, it's around me, and it's on the floor, too, Mommy!"

"That's wonderful, honey! Does it feel good to you?" I asked him.

"It's pretty cool, Mommy."

Somehow, I knew instinctively that by the end of the day, Keir would see light and aura everywhere. Keir described it as being all over the sidewalks and inside and outside people, too. According to some, Keir could see all seven levels of aura, including our surrounding personality colors, as well as the colors of our health that overlay the body. From that day on, he developed more specific tools for his own healing techniques. When a child had a "gray tummy," he'd send it energy until it turned green. A schoolteacher's headache was gray, and Keir changed it to green and then white.

I stood in the kitchen one morning while Keir ate his breakfast on the other side of the counter. "You know, your mother is standing next to you," Keir said.

I replied calmly, "Really, how do you know it's her?"

"Well, she answers to the name of Lois." I believed what my nine-year old said because he'd never known his grandma, and I always referred to her as my mom and not Lois.

"What's she doing here?" I asked him.

"I don't know. She's your guide. You figure it out! She's in the corner over there right now," and he pointed to the corner. How strange this was coming from my offspring who had never met his grandmother when she was alive. How would I deal with this child, when the child is a Master? In the course of a day, I never knew who was going to show up, the child who needed a parent, or the Master who is a remarkable teacher.

Mother

Twenty-two years ago, my mother lay in a hospital bed, hovering between life and death. For about ten days, she was in a coma-like state. She seemed to be holding on, unsure of what would happen next. I lay in a bed adjacent to hers. She was turned every two hours to prevent pneumonia, a two-person procedure. So my sleep pattern reflected that schedule and became what seemed like snippets of sleep between the moves.

One night, I got up around the 4:00 a.m. turning to sit with Lisa, the night nurse. We chatted a while, as we often did, at some point during the night. When the conversation ended, I got back into bed.

Then suddenly I heard, "Nancy." And I sat up in my bed because it was definitely my mother's voice, but she wasn't conscious. And then again, "Nancy." This wasn't her sick voice; this was her pre-illness voice, and I knew that firm tone all too well. I looked straight at her and her mouth was definitely not moving. She was still comatose. And then I heard her say, "Take the shoes from the shoemakers," or maybe it was, "Get the shoes at the shoemakers," I wasn't completely sure. And I said telepathically, "Okay, I will."

That was all. Not another word. I spent the next few hours trying to figure it out. That morning I called my stepfather's housekeeper and asked which shoes she had recently taken to the shoemaker. I had a feeling there were two pairs, one dark-colored pair and one light, which was confirmed by my stepfather's housekeeper. In that moment, I realized that the communication between us had been her final instruction to me, and that, in essence, she had told me what she wanted to wear at her funeral. Since she had no idea how long she had been between the worlds, she had left it up to me to decide how to dress her . . . depending on the season. To my mother, who was always impeccably dressed even to go to the grocery store, the information had been so important to her that it had transcended communication in this dimension.

One morning a few years ago, when I was upset with the relationship I felt no longer served me, I experienced the unmistakable smell of her perfume that came out of nowhere and hovered in the air for a minute or so. I hadn't smelled that for years. To this day, I continue to feel my mother's touch, hear her voice, and be comforted by her words.

Once I awoke from a nap when someone touched my thigh. And although I was surprised, I was also delighted because this was possibly the first time I had felt anything that I could call direct experience, or phenomenon, with a spirit on the other side. I had no doubt that it was Lois.

My mother had been a bacteriologist before I was born. She would take me to the serology lab of a former colleague, and I would do fake experiments with real vials of blood. I would watch the cells dance under the microscope. Those cells remind me of the activity within the balls of light I see over my head each night. That activity is similar to what lies within the cellular structure of our physical bodies. Both are visual examples of the flow of life. The distance between God and us is the same distance between us and ourselves. As above, so below; as within, so without.

The Psychic Lessons Begin

My closest friend Anne Bar-Tur died in 1983, the same year as my mother. She was the one who led me to develop my psychic ability. As a child, I had on more than one occasion been profoundly intuitive, and so had Anne.

We took our first classes together in psychic Frank Andrew's basement in SoHo, the area in Manhattan south of Houston Street, where I have resided since 1978. Eventually, we talked a mutual psychic friend into teaching us how to read cards, Italian ones similar to Tarot. I was uncanny at that. But there had always been a psychic connection between Lois and me, and I had stopped reading cards for people when she died. Everyone I read for before her illness had a sick and dying mother. I had not gotten that the connection was to my own life, and it was as if I had quit in protest.

Anne and I were always exploring the psychics, and she would send me off to whoever it was she had just gone to see. I remember a woman from Texas I had visited in New Jersey. It was my first experience of seeing someone channel. Anne told me she could see the man that this woman was channeling while she was doing a reading for her. I was anxious about going, and I wondered if I would be able to see that as well. I was so nervous about what I would see there that I had given myself a headache by the time I arrived, and there was no hiding an aching head from her. I didn't see the man that she became when she channeled, but I did see that the room she was sitting in had a particular light of its own. The entire space was filled with an ethereal glow unlike anything I had ever seen, and it was a remarkable sight I welcomed after Lois' death a month earlier.

My mother died of lung cancer at age sixty-two. She loved to smoke and had smoked several packs a day since she was a teen. In the months before her death, she had visions of both her parents. Now I know how comforting it must have been for her to see them.

My continuing relationship with my mother is the best proof to me that there really is no death. Yes, the physical body dies, but I have been personally shown so many times in the past few years that she is present and here for me—just on the other side of the veil. She was my biggest source of support as I grew up, and I am grateful that she continues to support me.

If only each of us could see our loved ones who have crossed over as they are now, beings in light on the other side. They constantly surround us, and when we access them through our own abilities or through another's, it serves as a reminder that, although we are here now, when our lives end and we become light, we are only a veil away from the continuum that holds all time and space. There really is no death, only breaks from the physical body—and sex and chocolate.

We may feel lonely, but we are never alone. It's always a crowded room. How would it change our relationships to each of our friends, family, and/or children just knowing that? There are those who advise us to parent our children just as if there are a dozen people watching. Well, there are! If we all open ourselves to access those other dimensions that are so close to some of us and so foreign to others, then we would all understand what an amazing place this Universe is.

Just Call Me Ray
August 18, 2005

Last night I got into bed too tired to stay awake for the "Mary and Blue Ball" show, now a nightly event. This morning, I sat Mary on the edge of my bathtub on one side of my large white bathroom. I closed the door and turned out the light, simulating the darkness of night. Soon, glow-in-the-dark Mary began to dance, and I asked for the blue energy to join me. In a few minutes, a ball of light formed in front of me, not so blue, but definitely composed of iridescent light. "What can I call you?" I asked. I'd been asking, but the names didn't feel right. Ray was what I heard now—short for Blue Ray—the frequency that Derek O'Neill talks about as the one being brought in to heal all disease on the planet now. More than one of them could then function as the Rays . . . or the Rayettes, for that matter! I asked how many there were, and I was told a few, in keeping with my request that there not be too many. If you woke up to several beings standing around, and you understood that you're ultimately the one in charge, you might want to empty the room out a little too! Two beings were fine with me, but they are the Christed Extra Terrestials (resonating to the Law of One), so three seemed to be the most appropriate number for them to have with me. I asked if the same beings were always there, and I heard that that wasn't important—better to think of them as a collective rather than individuals, so I could refer to all of them as Ray if I chose. "Name, fame, put in a frame. This is not the reason why we came."

CHAPTER EIGHT

THE LAND OF MERLIN

Keir wanted to go to Stonehenge from the time he was about five years old. I remember the first time he asked me when we could go there. I was putting him to bed one night, and I couldn't imagine how he'd even heard of it. Nor do I remember his explanation when I asked. He was insistent about going there, though, and I promised him that someday we would. From time to time in the next few years, he would remind me of this promise.

At the end of 1999, when Keir was ten, David and I were just finishing our commission for the London Millenium Dome, England's intriguing homage to the turn of the century. The commission was the first version of our Human Race Machine, which shows people how they look as a different race. Keir and I decided to go to London for the press opening of the Dome at the end of December 1999. It was an opportunity to take an extra day to go to Stonehenge, an hour-and-a-half drive from London by bus.

It was bitter cold in London, and on the day we had planned for our journey to Stonehenge, it began to snow. It snowed so hard that the bus tour was diverted from Stonehenge, and we spent the day at the town of Bath instead.

We were both disappointed, but we had a joyous adventure in that medieval, snowy place. We made two trips to Bath's gigantic cathedral that day, as Keir needed to spend more time there for some reason that I didn't even ask about. The bus driver knew how disappointed Keir was at not seeing Stonehenge, so on the way back that night, he stopped the bus and we all traipsed across the snowy highway to the icy fence that seals the state property off from the public. The driver of our bus had arranged with the night watchman of Stonehenge to shine his flashlight on the stones for us. We watched, looking through the angle of the heavy snowfall, as each stone was lit. I watched Keir's face reflect his letdown. We had come all this way, and this was the only view we got! He bit his lip, holding back his tears.

When we got back in the bus, I held his hand and told him that I didn't know why this had happened, but I knew that if we were really meant to be there, that Merlin would arrange it perfectly some day.

Merlin Journey

The first time Keir and I met and traveled with Meryl Beck was in 2000, just after my first experience with the Light Beings on Jodi's lawn at her country house. We agreed to travel to England because it was a trip advertised as a Merlin journey. Keir and I seemed to have a direct link to the Merlin consciousness, with Keir as "the channel," so this trip seemed tailor-made for us. Meryl had been to Starr's retreat center for the weekend, and Starr had called to tell me that we must go with this wonderful woman on the trip to England.

I hadn't traveled well during the years when I was sick, and even though I was feeling stronger, I was still reluctant to go anywhere. However, I was inspired by the idea of going on a Merlin journey and was determined to be just fine.

The plane was crowded, and I asked Keir where Merlin was, as I hadn't seen him. I usually noticed his presence as a patch of purple light whenever Keir was around.

"He's right there, Mom," Keir said, indicating that he was standing in the aisle right next to us, "and he's okay with not having a seat."

"Does Merlin like TV?" I asked Keir.

"Why do you ask?" he said.

"Because I always see him standing next to the TV."

"He's not watching TV, Mom. He's watching us watch TV!"

We planned to meet the rest of the group at Heathrow Airport in London, and from the moment we all met, we felt comfortable and welcome in the group's casual atmosphere. Meryl, our group leader, was especially kind, and she had a twinkle about her that was pixie-like.

As we boarded the purple "Merlin" bus to Cornwall, I saw that Keir was rereading his copy of *The Mists of Avalon*. He had an entire shelf filled with Merlin books, which he read and cherished. When we arrived six hours later, we were in a tiny coastal town called Tintagel. The hotel owner met us saying, "Welcome to Camelot." The name of the hotel was Camelot, and I wondered if this was the only place in the world where it's appropriate to greet guests in that manner.

The sea lay just beneath the hotel, and Merlin's alleged home, called "Merlin's Cave," is directly underneath. A few years earlier, excavations at Tintagel Castle next to the site had unearthed several ancient coins marked with an "A" (perhaps for Arthur). We were all giddy from the energy of the place. This was the first time we had ever been in a vortex of energy, and we had never experienced that energetic high before. It was as if we had all just smoked a joint, but even better.

Vortexes are concentrations of earth energies that occur at ancient monuments and sites where electromagnetic readings, measurable with scientific instruments, confirm heightened activity. There are only two significant energetic vortexes in the U.S. One is Sedona, Arizona, and the other is Mt. Shasta, California.

Keir was the only child in the group of about fifteen, but that never mattered. He bonded immediately with Alan, an energy psychologist and large child at heart. We'd been listening to Alan's stockpile of jokes all that day. He never seemed to run out. When we arrived at Tintagel, Alan pulled Keir over to a hill. He lay in the grass and proceeded to roll down one of the soft green hills. Keir followed suit, as did Meryl and a few others, while the rest of us stood by, laughing. We couldn't help but notice Meryl's totally infectious laugh, causing us all to laugh a lot harder. Keir and I were completely enchanted and grateful to be on what promised to be an amazing journey.

Before Keir and I went to sleep in our room that overlooked the sea, I felt dizzy and nauseated. I sent prayers to Merlin, asking him to please help me feel totally and completely well in this magical place called Camelot. I went to sleep and awoke to find a big ball of light coming toward me through the balcony window opposite our beds. As the ball got bigger and brighter, I was frightened and didn't move. Suddenly, a shaft of light came through the window and across the room, hitting me directly at my throat. Then another shaft followed, directing itself right over my head. This was truly an amazing sight, and I couldn't stop the tears of gratitude that were flowing from my eyes. I had never in my life seen anything like this. I didn't move. I felt it was truly a Divine manifestation of my prayers and proof that they had been heard.

I woke Keir so that I could have a witness to this miracle. He thought it was "very cool," but wanted to know if he could go back to sleep, since he had definitely seen it now and would absolutely recall that this wasn't a dream. I remember he asked me what I thought it meant, and I replied that I thought it was a healing. And looking back, it also felt like an initiation into that magical place that symbolized a new way of seeing. The white beams of light hovered at my throat and crown for about ten minutes until the ball of light from which they came faded.

The next morning, I awakened to a loud humming, a sound so loud I asked Keir what it was. He didn't hear anything. Then I realized that I was hearing for the first time the sound—the frequency—of the Earth. I opened the door to the balcony and stepped out. Yes, it was even louder outside. And in the course of the next half-hour, I realized that when I intended it, the sound became softer. I told Keir that the Earth sounds like a large, low-humming refrigerator!

That summer Keir kept borrowing my camera to take pictures of the fairies, but none showed up on the film. Keir tried to show them to all the rest of us, but he was the only one who could see them. In any case, when he "saw," he would see the entire being, whereas I would see a little light or color. When Merlin, or the Merlin consciousness, came to live with us, Keir would see his hat, his robe, the stars on this robe, and his whole face, whereas I would simply see purple shapes.

When our bus pulled into Marlborough for the first time, Keir immediately noticed the Fairy Store across the street from the hotel, and we went in. Looking around, Keir pulled me over to the small china figurines of the fairies. "Look Mom," he said. "I must not be the only one who can see the fairies, because these fairies are wearing the same outfits as the ones I saw!"

Shining Being

Keir and I first met Isabelle Kingston in 2000, during our "Merlin" trip. Isabelle is one of England's most revered psychics, healers, and Masters, who has never advertised. Full-figured, with her trademark blond mane of poofed hair, the enigmatic Isabelle developed her gifts early in life. With siblings who were much older than she and her father's death when she was five, her childhood was one of isolation. She would wander the fields by herself.

Isabelle recalls seeing the fairies as balls of colored light that she had experienced as a young child. Her only true teacher has been Merlin, and this consciousness and guide has been with her all of her life. With my eleven-year-old Keir by my side, our first conversation with Isabelle took place in a crop circle in Wiltshire and went something like this:

"So you're the young man I've heard so much about."

"I hear you channel Merlin." Keir replied.

"I hear you do too!" Isabelle responded.

It started to rain and, being English and psychic, Isabelle had brought an umbrella. I could hear Keir deep within the circle laughing with Meryl and some of the others in our group. I took a few pictures of Isabelle standing majestically under her huge umbrella, waiting for the summer sprinkle to pass.

"Your father was a particular challenge to you, wasn't he?" she asked me.

"Yes, he was," I said.

"He's learning a lot from you now, though."

This was amazing, I thought. Jodi had channeled my father a few months earlier, and those were the exact words she had used. The confirmation touched me deeply.

In the few days that followed, we got a crash course on Wiltshire's energetic vortexes that are located in the countryside northwest of London. Wiltshire is the area in which many of the Sacred Sites are found, including Stonehenge, Avebury, and Glastonbury. Silbury Hill, Europe's largest man-made burial mound that is several thousand years older than Stonehenge, sits just outside Avebury. The word "sil" derives

Silbury Hill, the "cosmic connector," Avebury, England, © 2003

from the words meaning "Shining Being," and Isabelle refers to it as the "great cosmic connector." To this day, Silbury Hill, or hill of the Shining Beings, remains one of my very favorite places in the world. The energy I feel from that place is magnetic. Standing on its top is always one of the highlights of my trips to Wiltshire. It is always a privilege to be there, and it feels as if I can recharge my batteries on that spot.

There are also many smaller energetic vortexes containing burial chambers called long barrows. The ley lines that cross at these sites also crisscross over England. These very powerful streams of energy are called the Michael/Mary lines. These can also be thought of as male/female or positive/negative in polarity. Take a stroll through the Glastonbury Abbey yard, which lies mostly in ruins from being burned by Henry VIII, and you can actually feel the lines of energy that cross there.

What the ancients knew was passed on to the Christians. The major sacred sites as well as each cathedral and abbey in England is aligned along the Michael/Mary lines. Even the center-points within the cathedrals line up according to the underlying path of geodetic energy that runs underneath them. Joseph of Arimathea accompanied Mother Mary here, so the legend goes, and planted a thorn tree. A descendent of that original thorn tree still stands on Wearyall Hill near Glastonbury Tor. It is also said that Jesus came to this land to study with the Druids. The Druids were closely related to the Magi, or Merlin, as represented by one of the three Kings that came to Jesus at the time of his birth.

The land in England is composed mostly of chalk and limestone, and when it heats up in the summertime, the energetic component of the land heats up as well. Between the energy of the ley lines and the energy of the sacred sites, which are all connected, it is a magical land where the veils between the dimensions are thinner, making the senses more acute. Those who access energy visually will see more energy. Those who hear messages will hear more, and the feelers will feel with more sensitivity. *In Seed of Knowledge, Stone of Plenty*, physicist John Burke writes about the effects of electromagnetic energy on seeds at these sites. He also says that the high level of energy acts as an inoculation against stress, producing more antioxidants that decrease the free radicals in the body. Vaccinated with energy, even the elderly in the area look incredibly vital.

Isabelle knows every crack in every stone from Stonehenge to Avebury and throughout England, so being in her presence is always magical. She teaches how to tune in to the stones, to feel their energy, and how to listen for them to communicate with us. Six months earlier, I held Keir's hand and told him that Merlin would arrange it perfectly if we were meant to be at Stonehenge. And Merlin had indeed arranged it perfectly. Because of our affiliation with Isabelle, and our journey to Stonehenge as part of a spiritual group, we were privileged to get sunset passes inside the stones. Spiritual groups, including the Druids that to this day perform ceremonies there, are allowed in for an hour apiece.

During our first time at Stonehenge together, Keir placed his forehead on a stone and was shown visions of all the sacred ceremonies there. I "heard" that the reason I was there was to bring Keir. It was the first of many similar messages I would hear in the sacred sites. Isabelle showed us the exact spot to stand while she brought down light to each of us as we stood on the secret, most highly charged spot in that mystical place.

Keir (age 11) and Isabelle at Stonehenge, © 2000

I still cherish a picture I took of Keir and Isabelle the first time they stood there together. Having stood on that spot numerous times now, I am always reminded of how connected we are, not only to this Earth, but to all that there is.

Healing Rays
August 27, 2005

Again last night, I played with the blue glowing balls on either side of me in bed. I'm feeling nurtured by them these days. I am an etheric juggler as I play with them and hold them in my hands. Whatever they've been doing in terms of my all-around health seems to be working. My digestion is improving, and the past few nights, I have felt them working on, or should I say inside, my head. I know the damage to my head (left side, near the front) is the result of a car accident in which a car grazed my head when I was about ten months old. My bonnet added just enough protection that I survived the accident. Over the years I have dealt with this energetic break in countless ways and on many healing tables. There has always been a bump there. In the past week, I have noticed that the shape of my head has changed in that area, and it feels now as if it's been strengthened.

In the past several nights I have felt the Rays go straight into my right ear to work on me. It feels odd, but I assume that they are consciously showing and allowing me to witness the process so that I will become an aware participant in my healing. The more I understand, the more I surrender through love. It is apparent to me now why they get so close to me. They are going inside of me for the purpose of healing me. Now they know me inside out! Sometimes, when they are in healing mode, a white mist forms around me. It is a cloud of energy that also carries a high-pitched sound along with it. I can't see through its density, yet it is the cloud cover that creates physical clarity.

Freddie Silva's book on crop circles, *Secrets in the Fields*, is a catalog of detailed information on both the controversies and science of the circles. Toward the end of the book, we read of Freddie's very personal experience in the fields. One night he was levitated by a group of tall white beings in a circle. The book also contains one of Isabelle's channelings that states contact with Universal beings is made with humans through the right ear. This continues to be my experience as well. There is a sound that signals their presence around me. The tone is very high-pitched, and I usually hear it on both sides of me, but sometimes for a few seconds, I feel it more intensely in my right ear.

CHAPTER NINE

THE DANCE OF LIFE

Derek O'Neill is the Avatar in my life, and he has been both friend and teacher to me. We met in 2002 long before I understood that his car runs on Love, not gas. He has a habit of testing generosity in his students by overshadowing homeless people (the technique for taking on the form of others) and then asking the students who encounter him for money. When his students fail to give him (the homeless person) money, they have flunked his test of generosity. Being in Derek's presence is nothing less than an exposure to boundless quantities of loving energy—for me it begs the question, exactly what would a reincarnation of Jesus be like?

When I went to Ireland for a weeklong workshop with Derek in June 2005, several people told me about a special statue of Mother Mary outside the church near the hotel in Tallaght, Dublin. Some of us went to see her, and as the serenity of her white stone glowed, we all watched in amazement as her face morphed into Jesus and then into Peter. Her arms appeared to extend to us, and her head moved from side to side. We watched this extraordinary apparition as it shifted and changed before us. Certainly I had never seen a statue do that before. In gratitude, we left her offerings of chocolate and flowers in exchange for showing us her gifts. Looking back, I could see that this was the first dancing Mother Mary we had ever seen. Even then I realized that this magical manifestation was brought to us by our loving teacher, The Irish Swami.

Mary dancing in my bedroom was multi-leveled and rich in meaning for me and symbolic of the celebration that is the dance of life. Some of the happiest moments I have ever encountered in this lifetime have been through dance. It's a practice I allow myself to do almost daily, because it is one of the best ways to alter a mood. From my first memories of dancing as a child atop my father's feet, I have always been passionate about dance. What I didn't know until just a few years ago is that dance has historically been the spiritual practice of women worldwide. To sit still and meditate is a masculine practice, while the feminine form of meditation is actually movement. Women are fluid, men are constant; women move, and men sit still. From the beginning of time, women danced as a ritual to call in the energies of God as their partner.

How is it that my glow-in-the-dark Mary can dance? How does she do that? I believe there is something about my energy that acts in conjunction with the Rays that propels her. As the days go by and she continues her evening dance, I still watch her as I fall asleep. When my energy is low, she paces instead of dancing. When I'm in a good mood, she dances so wildly that I'm concerned she's going to jump over the edge. When I engage her, she glows. When I disengage her, she goes out. Her mood and her moves definitely parallel mine. Therefore, it must be my energy that Mary is connected to. How could it be anything else?

Perhaps Mary is dancing because her secret is out. Like the Elohim, or creation energies, the Rays have been here from the beginning of time. It is the frequency of the Blue Ray that Derek says will act as a reverse vacuum for all human disease on the planet. It is their frequency of pure love that heals all and can change karmic patterning. Remember the blue angel Gabriel who came to Mary and impregnated her? It was the Elohim, in the form of the Blue Ray that seeded Jesus, Mohammed, Buddha, and the other Ascended Masters. Krishna was blue too. Now is the time for us to understand that Christ's conception arose from the same creation energies that seeded the human race, as well as the Masters. Could Mary be celebrating the arrival of the Rays? They have come now to be the teachers of cosmic consciousness. Maybe dancing Mary is one of those phenomena that starts small and then becomes a whole movement! In that case, glow-in-the-dark Mary could be a teaching tool connecting us to each other.

This is the planet on which we learn to be love, first for ourselves and then for each other. As long as one child in the world goes to sleep hungry, how well can we be doing? Our cosmic connectors are here, too, and they've come to help. I'm not alone. There are others who have asked them to be their teachers as well. All each of us has to do is ask, and they will come.

CHAPTER TEN

NIGHT SCHOOL

One aspect of Starr's work is called "night school." "Night school" is a euphemism for where we go when we leave our bodies at night. It takes place on the astral plane, where everything that ever was and is exists. Almost every spiritual teacher teaches on the astral plane, so nighttime is an opportunity to connect to whomever it is you are studying with. All you have to do is make an intention to connect with whomever you want to before you go to sleep and you probably will. Most of us do this nightly, although very few have any conscious memory of it. It tends to feel similar to a conscious dream state, yet it feels more interactive than actual dreams themselves.

For example, if you were a shoemaker who wanted to learn more about making shoes, you would spend your time on the astral plane learning from someone who teaches that skill. This is what a lot of us do at night. We continue the work we are already doing during the day. I usually meet the people whom I will be physically meeting within a day or two before our actual meeting. I meet them on the astral plane first, and then I know what to expect when we meet in reality.

When I first began to go to group meditations at Nancy Johnson's, I would occasionally feel myself leaving my body when I lay down to meditate. It made me queasy and kind of dizzy, and I didn't like the feeling that I had left my body and was suddenly moving upward. That has been my experience in both meditation and night school. Like most new things, it felt odd at first, but when you get used to it, it isn't nearly as strange.

After attending night school for a while, you begin to have some awareness of where you were or who was there with you. Usually a lot of people are around, and much of what I remember is just that—lots of people and lots of talking. With that knowledge and additional awareness of being out of my body, I developed a different relationship to sleep. I found I was dreaming less and flying more even when I napped in the afternoon. I'd see myself on an airplane and a flight attendant would approach me and say, "Do you want to go any higher?"

One thing I learned is that when things are possibilities, they are likely to occur on the astral plane first. You can eat whatever you want, have sex (although it's not appropriate to do that unless it's with someone who also wants to be with you), and visit with friends and loved ones on the other side. It's also a good opportunity to communicate with anyone you're in a relationship with, whether it is a child, a mate, a boss, or a friend. You can work out a lot of your mirroring of each other at night in order to have better communication during the day.

One of my favorite night school experiences took place the first time I went to Ireland with Isabelle Kingston. I had asked her what Master to be with at night, as this wasn't officially Merlin's territory. She told me to ask for the Goddess of the Boyne, since this was the Boyne Valley. Before I went to bed, I made an intention to meet her. I saw her standing by the Boyne River, and she put a leaf in my hand. "Look," she said, taking a cloud and placing it over the leaf. "You see," she said, "they're the same. They are one, as people are one." Then she showed me the range of emotions that all of us have as human beings. I felt it all, everything from pain to bliss in a courtroom in which I was the defendant sitting in judgment of myself. It was a reminder to me that our biggest job is learning to love ourselves.

Before 9/11, there were only hundreds of us who attended night school. Now there are millions. The significance of night school is enormous. It is potentially where the healing of thousands can take place and an opportunity to be of service even when you're asleep.

For example, after the Asian tsunami, we became a unified work force, guiding thousands of little children who died simultaneously into the Light. The tsunami was such a rare event, in which so many people died at the exact moment, and there was so much confusion and chaos—the event had unfolded so fast that most didn't realize what happened. All we night schoolers could do was be in complete service.

If the night school work we've done on any given night is particularly difficult, it's possible to wake up feeling physically "sore." That's the way my physical body felt after 9/11, the tsunami, and Hurricane Katrina.

Psychic Attack

Ever since Starr's college days she had worked with various government institutions who utilized her psychic abilities. Most notable of these was Project Foresight, a group formed by the military six months before 9/11, when seventeen Russian suitcase bombs went missing. Starr's clashes with the heads of the operation eventually led to her dismissal from this covert operation.

Then, in March 2004, she began to have what she classified as psychic attacks. She suspected these attacks were related to her differences with the heads of Project Foresight. They were characterized by a frequency going through her ear which initially shattered one of her ear drums. The attacks continued and increased in intensity, eventually affecting her brain and kidneys.

I felt that these attacks were just the beginning of attempts on Starr's life. In the past twenty years, radionics technology has blossomed. Steven Lewis, author of the book *Sanctuary*, was using similar technology to run particular frequencies across trays of photos of people in order to improve their health. When I attended one of his lectures, I asked what would happen if that same technology fell into the "wrong" hands. It would certainly be easy enough to adjust a frequency to affect an individual adversely as well as for health benefits.

In my experience I had used sound to facilitate my own healing. Sound is a key element in the Universe, and that is the reason it is such an effective tool for healing. It is also what makes Jodi's sounds so effective in shifting health. There is a tone, a frequency for everything from B complex to calcium to heroin. There is even a tone for orgasm. Everything resonates at its own frequency, including people. I had been told I was missing some tones in my aura, and was led to Sherri Edwards' work with tone. Sherri had conducted research with one of the universities and had invented a computer program that was used to provide the exact tones missing from people with chronic illness. Her studies showed that people could bring their weaknesses into balance by putting the sounds they were missing back into their energy fields. I went to one of Sherri's students and effectively filled in the frequencies I was missing with a little box of tones that were provided.

After Starr's most serious attack, I told her I was going to contact Derek. I felt it was the only alternative left, and she agreed. I called him immediately, and he told me not to be concerned. It was no problem, he assured me. He told me that it was all taken care of from that moment on.

The next night, Starr phoned me. She was standing at her kitchen window. She said she was looking out on the lawn and there were a thousand warriors in different battle regalia there to protect her. She hadn't felt any sort of attack all day. I emailed Derek to thank him, and he replied, "Those are the Knights of Light . . . all the Lads."

The next time Starr and Derek saw each other was at a gathering of metaphysical speakers at an outdoor event one night in L.A. I studied them carefully with the awareness that I was the only one who knew that a few months earlier, Derek had most probably saved her life.

We were all seated around one of the big round tables, and I took a picture of Derek and Starr as they sat close together sharing some private whispers. I had finally met Brook Still that day in Derek's workshop, and she was there too. My nephew Rick, my niece Mindy, and Libby, a friend of Mindy's, had also joined us. Libby handed Derek a little glow-in-the-dark Mary icon and asked him to bless it for her. He placed it between his cupped hands in prayer position. Derek held it for such a long time that I remember wondering what he was doing to that little statuette. Then he opened his hands and blew on Mary, slightly activating her happy glow. At that point, Mary was passed around the table for each of us to hold. I said I really wanted one of these, and Rick took me to get one the next day.

Don't Call Us Aliens
July 22, 2005

The Rays are as loving as loving gets. They love unconditionally, without an agenda. They are here with me all the time, seeing everything I do and hearing every thought I have, as all our guides are. Sometimes living with the Rays is as if I had my own team of cheerleaders who are always on my side. Their advice is divine. For example: "What allows us to move forward is the recognition that we are all fine just the way we are and that all is perfect the way that it is." And another example: "Forget regret. It binds you to the past. Move forward—look forward only, and let go of all the rest."

When they are serious I know it's because they are bringing me the bigger picture. "Don't call us aliens," they told me. "We are not alien to you. We are an integral part of you. We were there from the beginning, and we are still with you—connected by love. We've been here from the dawn of time."

CHAPTER ELEVEN

GROUP INTENTION

The second time I went to Jodi's country house was with Michael (my boyfriend at the time), Keir, and Alan Steinfeld, an expert on metaphysics. We went early in the summer of 2003 as a sort of preparation for our upcoming visit to the crop circles in England. As we drove up the driveway to Jodi's house, Michael took his new digital camera out of the box and shot a few pictures of Keir surrounded by orbs. Michael was in a state of shock when he saw the images, because it was a brand-new camera, and he knew it couldn't possibly have a defect. Alan explained that the orbs are a form of plasma energy, like lightning or the aurora borealis. But they seem to respond to intention, which would make them conscious.

Alan stayed behind while a few of us went into the woods. He was lying on the grass when he felt something behind him. He picked up his digital camera and took a picture of a huge, solid-looking orb. It was so solid it resembled a white pizza hanging in the sky.

Elated by what Alan had just captured on his camera, Alan, Jodi, and I gathered together to bring in the energy to capture more of this phenomena. Michael took pictures and kept shooting as Jodi began to channel sounds while the three of us formed a circle. To Michael's amazement, he captured a ball of light in a single frame among the three of us in a sequence of six images. These photos were published in my book, *Focus*. To Jodi, it was photographic evidence that what she does is real; the ball of light seemed to disappear between her hands.

About midnight, everyone went outside with the intention of bringing in the beings from Sirius that Jodi has brought in before, on that very spot. Keir and Michael were slightly apprehensive as the five of us lined up holding hands. Keir was in the middle, because he didn't want to be on the end. Jodi said some prayers and began to tone. Soon beings began to appear in a group about thirty feet from us. They appeared as a hazy mist of white. Alan, Jodi, Keir, and I saw and felt them, but Michael did not. We had been together about eight months by then, and he would periodically vacillate and waver on the subject of Spirit and then fall back on his former dogmatic belief system that nothing exists. Jodi was translating for the group. She said, "They are saying that they're appearing in a group this time because they want to convey a message of oneness to us. It's not that individuals are unimportant. What is more important now is that we bond together as a group consciousness as an example for humanity on the Earth at this time."

I inquired about the red streaks of light that I was seeing and that I'd seen before when Jodi and I had done this. Jodi said, "They're saying that's their energy." I asked, "If we sit down, would they get closer?" The answer was no, because when we sat down, the beings also sat down and they were too short to be seen. So we all got up again. "So much for intergalactic protocol!" I said. Michael, frustrated at seeing and feeling nothing, asked Jodi to ask them if there was another way to communicate. When Jodi asked if there was a different way all of us could experience them, suddenly there were music notes that seemed to come out of nowhere. It sounded like a toy piano, scales played that were not really scales, faint metallic sounding notes that had no real rhythm. The notes were clearly coming from our left side, and Alan asked if there was a house over to our left that had a piano. Jodi replied there was a house there, but she didn't know if they had a piano. She had been there seven years and had never heard anything from that house.

Meanwhile, Keir and I were seeing a multitude of colored lights, flashing on and off in the distance just like *Close Encounters*. Now the sound that had begun on our left began to come from our right side.

We were all talking at once, disagreeing with each other about what the sound was, although we all knew the direction of it had changed. Suddenly, each of us felt the same thing, and all our chattering and arguing stopped. Everyone was quiet. It was as if the sound was coming from both sides, inside our heads now, and there was some sort of vibration that met in the middle of our heads. We all had this experience simultaneously, even Michael, and we knew it wasn't a piano vibrating at the center of our heads. It lasted a few seconds, after which no one said a word. And then we came to agree that we no longer thought it was a piano.

CHAPTER TWELVE

INDIGO CHILD

By 1998 my loft had turned into a sort of healing salon where classes were given, meals shared, and meditations were conducted. I began to give parties—soirées really. Singing and dancing became more and more commonplace, and my home became a powerful healing vortex.

It was during one of these parties that my nine-year-old became a channel. I remember catching a glimpse of Keir as he suddenly appeared with a mustache and beard applied to his face in black marker. He put a sign up outside his room. The sign said, "Dr. Cranberry is in session. 25 cents for 5 minutes."

"What's going on?" I asked him.

I'm doing sessions," he told me. "Dr. Cranberry," he explained, "was a psychologist who lived somewhere in Europe." And with a "client" in tow, he went into his room and closed the door. Soon a line of people formed outside of his room, and I was watching the looks of amazement on the "clients" leaving. I grabbed Jodi, who has channeled regularly for years, and asked her to investigate. Was he really in channel? I wanted to know the inside story of what was going on in my nine-year-old's space in the midst of eighty guests in our loft.

Eventually Jodi came out, smiling brightly. "What's going on in there?" I asked.

"There's a lot of Merlin energy in one corner, and he says there's a psychologist from Europe named Dr. Cranberry coming through him, and the energy in the corner is connected in as well."

I saw Starr go into Keir's room. Someone had been holding her place in line. Five or ten anxious minutes went by before she came out and said, "Your son is awesome. He's an incredible healer and a great presence . . . an indigo with many talents and abilities in metaphysics. I honor you for being the mother of this Master in child's form."

When I saw Starr the next day, she told me that she had asked Keir how to get along with children better. He had answered that it was as if she had her foot on the accelerator and was giving it too much gas. His advice was to slow down a little. Take her foot off the accelerator and approach children at a slower pace. For the next several years, Keir appeared as Dr. Cranberry at many gatherings, with a line of people waiting outside his room. Eventually, he was making three dollars to answer three questions. I never really got a formal session. All I was told was that it didn't look to him like his dad was going to come back. That, I knew was the child Keir's human wish.

When he changed schools and developed new friends at age ten, he also formed his first close friendship with a girl. She was inconsistent, periodically treating him in a way that was uncomfortable, and he watched her treat others in a similar fashion. One day he told me that he saw a valve over her heart. The valve had appeared like a circular line around the parameter of her heart, and he could tell when she was going to drop a friendship, because the line indicated a reversal of energy in her heart. I told him that if he could see all that, then he had truly been given some of the most amazing gifts, as Keir's ability to see energy would clearly mean few surprises in love.

CHAPTER THIRTEEN

INSIDE THE CIRCLE

At the end of July 2003, Jodi, Keir, Michael, Meryl, and I went to Wiltshire to work with the energy of the crop circles and to hang out in Isabelle's presence for a week. Since we'd "practiced" that night at Jodi's house a few weeks before, we were all pretty much prepared for anything. On the plane, I showed Jodi an image that I had drawn of a hexagon. She asked if it was an image that had come from inside or outside my head. We sometimes kidded each other about those "incoming messages." A psychologist had once asked her whether the messages she receives come from inside or outside her head. "Inside," she replied. "That's good," the psychologist said. "Why is that?" Jodi asked. He told her that the messages from outside our heads are the ones that are related to serious mental illness, like paranoia or schizophrenia. In general, if the messages come from inside one's head, they're considered "normal" and not potentially harmful to oneself or others.

The week sped by magically, filled with the energy of the crop circles, the sacred sites, the hum of the Earth, plus the vortex of Wiltshire as shown to us through Isabelle's teachings. When Isabelle channeled the Merlin Consciousness for us, Michael became concerned about why he was there. Michael always wanted to see more, but it seemed

Nancy and Jodi Serota in Glastonbury, England, © 2003 Michael Julian Berz

that the more he saw the more he shut down. During his first visit to my studio eight months earlier, he'd not only seen my aura, but my face in the future as well as my past. What about those spectacular shots of orbs and balls of light he captured at Jodi's country house? Why was he allowed to get those pictures? Even with the "doubting Thomas" that Michael's presence represented, there were a few occasions Michael found miraculous that trip.

The first came when we were all standing in a crop circle under the hottest English sun, as there was a massive heat wave that summer. There was absolutely no wind until Isabelle said, "The Archangel Michael always brings the wind." Suddenly, a huge gust of wind came from nowhere and continued blowing across the wheat until we left some minutes later. It was impressive to Michael because he had been filming in "the pit" on the first anniversary of 9/11. While the families of the victims were all in attendance, a wind had blown up downtown that was uncanny, and the wind at the crop circle that day reminded Michael of that experience. It had almost disrupted the services being held on the site when the huge American flag that hung from the Deutsche Bank Building tore in two. I also remember the sudden

Nancy, Isabelle Kingston, Jodi Serota and Meryl Beck, Salisbury, England, © 2003 Michael Julian Berz

severity of the wind that afternoon as I walked through SoHo thinking about what that moment must have been like for those assembled at the World Trade Center site.

One other manifestation came while Isabelle channeled Merlin for us that week. She told us that Merlin would appear to each of us in our rooms in the hotel in the form of butterflies. For Michael and me, the butterfly had already appeared on our first day. I was thrilled when I saw it, recognizing it as an angelic messenger from my books of animal totems. I grabbed my camera and took its picture, talked to it sweetly, acknowledged it, blessed it, and thanked it as the Merlin Consciousness, before gently escorting it back out the window. And, one by one that week, a butterfly had indeed appeared inside each of our rooms.

I was reluctant to leave after spending all week in the crop circles and Sacred Sites of Wiltshire. I took so many shots of orbs on my camera wherever we went, proof to me that though they may be a form of plasma energy like lightning, they also are a form of consciousness. Each time I picked up my camera and intended them to be there, they showed up, as if to say "You called us and we're here." The Universe does hear. The Universe hears everything and all things.

Bert Jansen's film, *Contact,* features the documentation of an experiment some Japanese researchers did in 1999. The team set an intention to create a crop circle by asking for the appearance of one on a specific night and in a specific place. They also asked that the symbol be of Japanese origin. What they got was a crop circle in the center of the area they had intended on that exact night, which looked like Japanese origami.

Our last night, we convinced Isabelle to come and sit in a crop circle with us. After so many years of all of her experiences, it was rather passé to her. Jodi, Isabelle, Michael, Keir, and I went to a "key" crop circle at West Overton Field. It was fairly accessible at night, in that it wasn't such a long distance out in the fields. We arrived at dusk. As the sun began to set, I got incredible photos of a field active with orbs. Then suddenly, there were no orbs at all, but simply a bright blue hexagonal shape hanging in the sky. In an instant, it was gone, documented by two shots I had taken, one with the hexagon and one without, but both with Keir's foot in one corner. Michael wondered why he couldn't capture the orbs anymore. Isabelle said, "Because cameras have consciousness, and you are perhaps . . . just a tad less open than you could be."

"Then why was I getting orbs at Jodi's house and not here?" Michael asked.

Well," Isabelle said, "it might have been what's sometimes called the

Blue hexagon from The Hand of God crop circle at West Overton field, © 2003

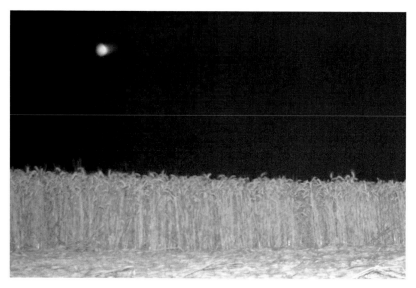

Ball of light at The Hand of God crop circle, © 2003 Michael Julian Berz

carrot to catch the donkey. You were shown a few things to sort of whet your appetite to discover more. It might be time for you to believe without the actual proof you're seeking."

It was quite dark when a truck that had spotted us stopped about a mile away. They probably expected that we were a team of hoaxers. It was a perfect opportunity for Michael and Keir to pretend they were "aliens." They put on their headgear (with flashlights atop) and jumped around the circle. Jodi added the vibrational languages to accompany the antics, and Isabelle prayed she didn't know the farmer of this field if we got caught. At this point, the guys in the truck had climbed on the top and had probably used some binoculars to realize it was simply humanoids having a good time. Crop circles are always great for getting giddy. You can get just as high on energy as you can on any drug.

Isabelle shared a story with us that befit our mood. She'd once had dinner with a man she was interested in enough to at least dine with him when asked. After dinner, they decided to wander a bit, and they went for a walk along the hills of Wiltshire. While they walked and chatted, a big blue ball of light appeared in the distance coming toward them. The blue ball continued to approach them, and as it got closer, it appeared to be about two feet high. Then it came even closer, until, finally, it was hovering directly across from both of them. Isabelle's date passed out, and she continued to enjoy the communication with the ball of light for a few seconds until it suddenly took off, vanishing on the horizon. She picked up her date and helped him back to his car. Not a word was spoken between them. When Isabelle got back in her car, she burst out laughing. Clearly, this one would never have understood her, and God had showed her the evidence of that immediately.

When the truck drove away, we took an assessment of all the activity in the field. I could see the orbs and other brighter globes of light that looked to me like the balls of light Isabelle had described. Michael did get a shot of one by putting his camera on automatic. He set it on a tripod, and it was shooting every thirty seconds. There was a kind of wheelbarrow of light that we watched that made Keir feel uncomfortable as it crossed the field. He was ready to leave after that.

I insisted we stay and do some intention through sound. So with Jodi in good voice, we said prayers and made an intention for the formation of a crop circle. We left around midnight.

By 7:00 the next morning, the circle at West Overton field had been

The Hand of God crop circle, © 2003 Steve Alexander

The Hand of God with extension at West Overton field, © 2003 Steve Alexander

extended the entire length of the field. We didn't hear about the extension of "our" circle at West Overton until a week later on the Internet. Ironically, it seemed to be a parting gift from the Universe, and I was particularly ecstatic, because it was, in a sense, another "carrot to catch the donkey." I was determined to come back again the next year and have a closer encounter with the balls of light. If we could assist in manifesting a crop circle, surely we could manifest the balls of light. Scanning through the archives of the Crop Circle Connector (the zenith of crop circle sites) years later, I discovered that small "key" circle had been named The Hand of God.

Robbert van den Broeke

I met Dutch researcher and video-maker Bert Jansen in a crop circle in England in 2004. We had a conversation about Robbert van den Broeke, a Dutch intuitive who has been communicating with the balls of light in the crop circles outside his home for many years. Robbert is the young man that Nancy Talbot, foremost crop circle researcher and head of BLT Research Team, Inc., has been working with in Holland. Nancy, along with biophysicist William Levengood and physicist and researcher John Burke, formed the BLT Research Team, Inc., in 1992. Their preliminary research findings were funded in 1999 by Laurence Rockefeller, which enabled them to continue with in-depth studies of the soil inside and outside the crop circles.

Robbert sees the balls of light. They had come to him in a crop circle right beside his home. In fact, he and Nancy witnessed three examples of circles formed through the creation of plasma vortexes striking the land in powerful tubes of light outside Robbert's house in August 2001. Talbot described them as terrifying, because they had struck the Earth with incredible force. The incident had been the first credible eyewitness account of the making of a crop circle, ironically, by the most respected researcher on the subject. It came just after Nancy complained loudly that there had never been any tangible proof of the phenomenon, thereby creating a mockery of her reputation and her career. Therefore, she was giving up and going to bed. Three plasma vortexes struck the Earth about fifteen minutes later, creating three crop circles.

Robbert has seen and photographed the balls of light on a regular basis. Bert Janssen's film, *Contact,* showed how the balls of light hit his

A photograph of a blue being, © Robbert van den Broeke, The Netherlands

house, scorching the wood. Then the balls of light had moved inside Robbert's house that he shared with his parents and sister. One day, Robbert saw a ball of light pull apart into a stream of light, come back together and pull apart again. Then the light stream came together and appeared as a small white being. Since then, Robbert has been allowed to photograph them consistently.

When I saw one of those images on the Internet for the first time a few years ago, I knew that it was real. I realized how easily it could have been created or altered with Photoshop. But, no . . . this was real; it felt real.

For me, that image was verisimilitude, the true appearance of God, versus similitude, the resemblance of God without the truth. And I thought, if this were the first time I was looking at a human face, I would probably think it looked odd. Our human eyes are trained to look for human beauty, but who am I to judge what beauty is within the context of the Universe? The Universe has no concept of deformity. Who are we to judge what beauty is and is not?

I remember the episode of *The Twilight Zone*, called "Eye of the

Beholder," in which a "beautiful" human is being operated on by other beings. We only hear what they are saying, and they are referring to her human face as ugly. The camera pulls back to reveal what the beings in control actually look like, and they are what most humans would call "ugly." Like my photos taken between 1991 and 1997 of craniofacial kids and adults with facial prosthetic devices from surgeries, the episode directly addresses the issue of beauty versus deformity.

I had learned a lot from my subjects during the years I had been privileged to photograph them. They taught me about self-love by being the Masters of the art of self-acceptance. In truth, our image of self is dependent on how we feel about what we see when we look at ourselves in the mirror on a daily basis. Self-acceptance and self-love is the constant challenge of being in a human body.

Robbert is allowed to photograph the ETs, but when I was in Wiltshire during the summer of 2005, I wasn't. Nancy Talbot, shooting photos in the same room with Robbert and at the same time, did take shots of the white and yellow beings, but the images were deleted from her disk, just as the phenomena I had photographed had been.

In 2004, Amsterdam television had called Robbert's house and arranged with his father, a banker and his personal manager, to bring their still cameras there. The news crew came and Robbert took photos of the beings. Since then, he has made many live appearances on Dutch television, showing viewers instantly that he can and does consistently take pictures of the beings around him. He will even take cameras from the audience to show that nothing has been set up, and that they are real. His father's book about the beings was at the top of the Dutch bestseller list in 2006.

From the moment I saw those pictures of Robbert's on the Internet, the balls of light made more sense. Of course, beings are inside of them; beings that are composed of light. They split apart. It all made perfect sense.

At the height of my interest in shooting orbs, I went to Maui. I wasn't sure whether I should go, but my guides told me to "go for the UFOs." My first night in the magic that is Maui, I stood outside setting an intention to capture images of the orbs. I shot photo after photo, said prayer after prayer, and not a single orb showed up. Downloading them from the camera later revealed more than I realized, as I had taken many shots of UFOs.

Knowing that Maui is an energetic vortex and that one of the highest concentrations of energy within that vortex is Haleakala Crater, I found a guide, and a few of us spent a full day hiking eight miles down and back from the center of the crater. It is the quietest place I have ever been. At the bottom of the crater lies a triangular volcanic rock that the locals say is a portal for UFOs. I took more photos of the UFOs down there and tangibly felt the presence of a few tall beings who walked with me, guiding my way back up the crater in the dark. I asked for and received more moonlight to brighten the stones, which then lit each step. The volcanic rock and mist made the hard, wet path a challenge, and the tall beings became my etheric taxi upward.

Divine Setup

It was from the Rays that our souls and personalities were spawned. Being fully aware of the Divine Plan, the Rays know each soul's mission. Understanding their omnipotence, I can clearly visualize the Divine setup placed in motion long before my birth. Let's find a human who is really familiar with deformity and who deeply believes in the beauty of all humans. If she can accept us, perhaps that would allow more humans to open to us. Pick someone who is close to Spirit, who loves God, who needs healing, who constantly asks to see, and who has invited us to share her home.

Is there a difference, other than visually, between the Rays and the balls of light? The balls of light become the Rays when they break open. When they first come in, they appear as tiny glimmers of white, blue, purple, or red light, and sometimes they can appear larger. They are very bright. That's what I see, and that's what others see. When they break open or morph, they turn a variety of colors, revealing themselves as sentient beings.

There is a difference between the Rays that are here with me and the beings that Robbert photographs in Holland. Robbert photographs beings of light that have heads and bodies. The Rays are beams (be-ams). They are slices of the light stream that is every color of ray. The slices puff up and become balls of light, and those balls of light are beings. The Rays are sentient, highly intelligent beings that can have faces and necks, but no bodies. Both groups are ETs; however, the Rays are spirit and energy, and the other ETs are spirit and corporal bodies. They are both what Derek O'Neill refers to as the Christed ETs that resonate to the Law of One. The Rays are part of the Elohim, the DNA specialists that designed the human form. The Elohim provided the physical bodies and electro-magnetics. The Rays provided the unvisible parts, the souls, and the personalities. The Elohim and the Rays are both aspects of God, and they are our celestial, angelic parents who gave birth to us.

The Ascended Masters like Jesus, Mohammed, Buddha, and Krishna were designed specifically to assist in creating consciousness and understanding on our Earth. They were special experiments, super beings to serve as exemplary models for God-consciousness on the planet.

My First Thoughts
August 20, 2005

For the last several nights, the messages that I have awakened to have been quite clear. I am asking the Rays for messages that I can understand, and if I don't receive what is being communicated instantly (as if we're in conversation), I'd appreciate it if they could please convey the information they want me to have as my first thoughts upon waking. That way, I avoid any ego attachment to what's being communicated, leaving the information uncorrupt. What I've heard repeatedly in the past few months is that I'm receiving lessons in truth and trust. I must trust myself, I'm told time and time again. I must trust that I can convey my truth and be heard. "Am I holding myself back?" I ask. Only I can hold myself back, and I am held back when I don't surrender in trust. I must also fully know that the Rays are here for my highest good, not only for my own healing, but because of the information that's being conveyed in this book.

Truth and Trust

Once when the Rays came to me in their usual nightly procedure, I became nauseated and very uncomfortable in my body. I kept waking up in response to the energy that was coming through me, and I remarked aloud that it was pretty rough going tonight. Must be a new level we reached. I fell asleep at last and was once again grateful for the messages that came through, the continuing messages that are lessons of truth and trust.

When I awoke, I saw myself already writing down what was being said while I simultaneously saw it in book form. In fact, it was already in this book. The message was such a profound moment in my relationship with God that I began to weep, enveloped in the understanding of their acknowledgment of my love for them. They had said:

"There has never been a way to show how much I love God than this that is happening right now."

And again this morning I was given an image of myself being physically shaken by someone, and I heard, "Let your confidence and belief be unshakable. Therefore, let nothing shake you." And on a different level, I thought of how much, in an effort to heal my body completely of any and all immune problems, they are vibrating my organs now—literally shaking them to resonate with the frequency of health.

The levels of meaning from Source are profound, funny, poignant, and often very ironic, as I viewed this message to be. They shake me constantly for purposes of aligning my health and simultaneously ask that I remain unshaken. Divine humor! No wonder laughter is so healing.

Inevitable

With so much public attention on a possible U.S. government cover-up, it does seem inevitable that our government will someday disclose that decades ago, they made a deal with certain groups of ETs: an exchange of people to serve as human experiments in return for the ETs' advanced military technology.

I want to be absolutely clear here, because there have been other times when groups of ETs visited Earth, and those groups weren't here for our highest good. However, I do believe that time is in the past, and that the Christed ETs here now come from the highest vibration of love with the sole intent of assisting mankind on its journey toward consciousness. If you want to ask for them to come to you, specifically ask for those beings only, as that is the only appropriate frequency to connect with. They are here to heal us emotionally as well as physically.

If we were going to a party and thirty people were going to be there,

there'd be a few humans in the room we didn't like, as well as a few others we really wanted to know better. Some people we simply resonate with better than others. The same is true with all our relationships within the Universe. We create our own realities in the realms beyond Earth as well as in our relationships here.

This is what the Rays channeled to me concerning those who have been abducted by ETs. "It is true that there have been others here as we are now, and their actions have been mercenary. Those of you who were chosen to have contact with them have been given some of the hardest lessons in this lifetime. And because these experiences have come to you, you have closed your hearts. When the heart is closed, the lesson that opens it is love, and that love is packaged in the form of forgiveness. The package itself, the pain, the hurt, is surrounded by love, but the contents are too dense for that love to penetrate. Until you can reduce the size of the package of pain and convert it to love within your heart space, you will remain without the God aspect that will place you in God consciousness. These specific experiences you have chosen as part of your life's path—your journey in this lifetime. If you fail to reduce your pain—if you fail at forgiveness of the imperfect Universe—you will remain at odds with God and man—standing between them as victims of the Universe's misunderstandings and mistakes. We love you as you are, but it's time now to reach for the most Divine forgiveness in order for you and us to move forward. Know that we are with you on this journey and that this was your soul's choice and decision. We love you and we are waiting to be loved in return. This is your challenge. Let it begin now."

If you should decide to ask the Christed ETs to be your healers, know that they, in return, will ask something from you. In exchange for your healing, what will be required of you is precisely this: Live in your hearts in truth and integrity, knowing that God lives within you always. Your mission then is to be an exemplary model of conscious understanding and love in every possible moment for the rest of your lives.

If you're ready to ask for the Ray's divine guidance, I would also suggest you find a teacher. All of us need appropriate teachers to accompany us on our bold journey from I to we. My highest recommendation would be to plan a trip to Ireland and visit an Irish Swami.

Color-full
September 9, 2005

Each night I turn out the light and wait for the flashes or streaks of light that come in just before the Rays appear. My home is their home now too, I thought to myself, although wondering whether or not they ever sleep or need to rest. In any case, they live here too. They had accepted my invitation. I asked them to come, and they did because they knew that I returned the love they had originally sent to me. They appear in all of the colors of the spectrum in order to make the same statement; there is no reason to distinguish among the colors. It doesn't matter. Faith is faith. Color is color. Both come in many forms no matter what we believe in. All Rays are the same color, even though they are different. I love to watch them as they change colors. They are all awakenings. If we spin all the colors of the Rays together in light, they become the rainbow of light. Just as the peacock, which symbolizes the Avatar, displays its array of different colors, when I see a being of the highest light, such as an Ascended Master, I see that energy as a rainbow of light.

Surrender

I put a Post-it note up on my refrigerator with the word "surrender" on it. To surrender is a concept I've learned from Derek O'Neill, and it has been the hardest for me to grasp. To let go is to admit that we alone are not in complete charge, at least not necessarily from the point of view of the biggest picture. Although we are responsible for our reality in every way, ultimately, all we can do is know that Divine Will exists as well and that everything is perfect just the way it is—no matter how bad it feels, no matter how bad the circumstances are; it's all perfect. Every curve ball is an opportunity to grow; that includes 9/11, tsunamis, and hurricanes, which I believe were allowed to happen as wake-up calls. When catastrophes happen, they grab humanity's attention. Disasters foster our compassion.

If they really are here, then why don't they "land," I'm asked. They'll only come when they'll be accepted by everyone, and the only way that will happen is when mankind agrees to stop killing each other and to feed everyone on our planet.

There is no reason every child in the world can't be fed and provided with shelter and medical care. As humans, we must take care of our own, no matter where we live, no matter what our skin color or faith. When the human body is dissected, it's all the same inside. How ready can humans be to accept the Rays when we can't even accept each other's skin color? We "hue-mans" of multicolored hues are all one. Unless we deeply understand this truth from the core of our own self-love, we can never arrive at the conscious understanding that we are all connected.

The reason Derek is such a hard teacher for me is that he knows how to bring up my stuff, my anger, and my ego. If I react when he tests me, it's the part of me that's out of alignment with my true God self. As Derek says, "The truth will set you free, but first it will piss you off."

Whoever or whatever we're fighting about is where we're out of alignment with God. Anyone and anything we're uncomfortable with has something to teach us. If we visualize each person we know standing directly in front of us, how much love do we have for that person? And how much judgment? Where we judge is where we separate from love and from God. It's a concept that appears so simple, so divine! We hold onto it for an instant or a few, and then it's gone again. It's an example of the ins and outs of conscious understanding. It's the moment that happens when we're walking down the street and suddenly enlightenment strikes. And there we are. We've got it all, complete understanding of everything. And then, by the time we reach the end of the block, we're wondering how late we're going to be if we miss the subway we now hear arriving directly underneath us. A few seconds ago, or maybe a few moments, everything was perfect just the way it was. And now that consciousness is gone, and we're simply running to catch a train.

Derek doesn't give you what you want. He gives you what you need to grow your relationship to yourself and God. He rarely answers questions directly, but sometimes he tells you what he thinks you want to hear. That doesn't mean it's the appropriate answer, it is only the answer in that moment. That doesn't mean he doesn't know what will happen next. He knows full well. But if he gave you the answer you're looking for, it might be undoing your karma, and that might not be what's meant for him to do in any given moment. It's what sometimes makes it difficult to distinguish between the swami and the leprechaun.

Sai Baba

There are plenty of photos of Sai Baba, Derek's teacher, around my home. He is a Purna Avatar, which means he can create something out of nothing. He's built two hospitals in India, which offer free medical care to all and are staffed by volunteer doctors from all over the world. He has the ability to shift karma instantly and has also shifted thousands of lives that would have ended in a split second. So if ever you're thinking that, for whatever reason, your life may end in the next few seconds, I wouldn't hesitate to call his name, as that is all it takes to shift your karma. Truly his contribution to India and the world is unique. Although I've never been to India, I've seen Sai Baba and felt his energy in my bedroom vortex, and I have seen him come through my pillow as well. He has also personally invited me to India, and I know someday I'll accept his invitation. Sai Baba says, "I am God . . . and so are you."

Blue
August 23, 2005
One night I asked the balls of light, "Why are you blue?" and I heard, "Because blue is your favorite color." As I watched the blue swirl of light, it came toward me nearer and nearer until it seemed as if it was completely engulfing my face. Within the mass of blue, there are sometimes what appear as black holes that I regard as likely to be eyes. I'm not afraid anymore. I only feel privileged. As the swirl of blue moved to one side of me, I held out my hands cupped in the air. It was my invitation to be present there. Soon, I held a mass of their blue-prickly-warm energy between my hands. I don't know how any experience I've ever had could be more profound than the ability to hold the Universe in my hands.

CHAPTER FOURTEEN

EIGHTH DIMENSION

At some point, I'd gone to see Starr teach her Dimensions class. That night she taught us how to access the seventh, eighth, and ninth dimensions. The seventh dimension is of light and color in which one can see different aspects of aura. In the eighth dimension, one can access past lives. In the class, we actually practiced accessing these dimensions with various partners. The ninth dimension is the Angelic Realm, and if you are really good at seeing energy, you can access that one as well.

I went home that evening and built a vortex for the eighth dimension in my bathroom and became a witness of my past lives in my bathroom mirror on a nightly basis. There are so many people, all a part of my soul, whom I accessed in that mirror. I've seen myself as children and the elderly of both sexes. I've seen myself deformed and blind. I've also seen myself as ETs, including a cat-like woman, a pig-type man, and a tall guy with a very high forehead. As one moves between lives, one's face goes blank, and there are no features at all.

It was a new level of knowing, and I quickly learned that we've all been so many people, some "beautiful" and others not, some human and some not. What an empowering thing to discover in one's bathroom mirror! Let's just throw out our present concept of beauty and expand it into knowing that it's not about what we look like, it's how we love, and how we're in service in this lifetime. It is another example that when our vision expands, we can glimpse the bigger picture. I saw Derek in the eighth dimension once. He looked like Christ to me, and he looked like a yogi as well.

Our souls have had thousands of lifetimes. Seeing is believing. How profound to be able to visually access everyone I had ever been. Clearly Earth has not been my only home.

CHAPTER FIFTEEN

HEAL ME

It was before the trip to Wiltshire in the summer of 2004 that I had made an intention to ask the beings, balls of light, or whatever energy was creating the crop circles, to come and heal my immune system. What I needed was a real miracle, and I wasn't sure that one was possible in the context of all I know about energy on Planet Earth. So when I asked that the circle makers heal me, it was with my knowing that there are frequencies in the Universe that are more powerful than those here on Earth. My message to the Universal God Consciousness was if my health issues are really to be resolved in this lifetime, I would surrender in trust, knowing that the time had come. It would be a form of Divine intervention and would make me capable of eating larger quantities of food and absorbing it better.

Michael, Jodi, Meryl, Keir, his friend Cam, and I all stayed at the Parklands Hotel that first week, a short distance from Marlborough. Our first night there, I woke up startled at having heard what sounded like nothing less than a huge electrical appliance—or a ship—landing right outside the window. I was terrified, and I gripped Michael's arm as he slept next to me. I remember thinking, okay, I promise if whoever you are comes back tomorrow night, I'll have the nerve to go to the window and investigate what's outside, but right now, I'm staying right here, because I'm too frightened to move. With that, a surge of energy swept over my body from my head to my feet. It had an intensity and heat that wasn't like energy I'd ever felt before, and I knew that this had been a real experience with energies not of this Earth. It wasn't the first, though. There was that vibration that had gone through all our ears and met in the middle of our heads outside Jodi's house. There had been one other dialogue on the lawn of Jodi's home in upstate New York, but in those situations, Jodi was right next to me. And this time, I'd asked for a healing and had received it all on my own. I understood what had happened to me, but I didn't recognize it enough to integrate it on a deeper level that this was my new, rather unreal reality. I asked the circle makers for a healing and they had actually come to me.

In June 2004, I had received visions, as precognitive gifts from Spirit, a month before my second trip with Jodi to the crop circles. I awoke one morning to a vision of a tiny human in a field. He was very small, and there was wheat growing up all around him. He had a baton and was wearing a tuxedo. It was as if he were conducting an orchestra in the field. It seemed to me like something was going to occur that had to do with sound, which really thrilled me because it was so meaningful that Jodi was again joining us. The second vision was of three people standing in a circle. One was me, one was Jodi, and Jodi and I couldn't figure out who the third person could be. I knew that Keir and his friend Cam weren't going to be with us that night. I was disappointed because I knew they were going to miss something significant. The three of us (including the person we didn't yet know) were standing in the field wearing fairy costumes with magic wands, and there were balls of light dancing between us. Michael, I felt, would be off in the distance.

The crop circle some were referring to as the Sun and Moon had landed in July, about ten days before our visit. Unfortunately, this same crop circle was used to recreate a fake one for a National Geographic special filmed later that summer. Not far from Avebury, West Kennett Long Barrow is an ancient burial chamber we had visited several times. It lies directly across from Silbury Hill. Both of these ancient sites are thousands of years older than Stonehenge. Isabelle describes West Kennett Long Barrow as a place where the tall beings lived, worshiped,

The Sun and Moon crop circle, West Kennett Long Barrow and Silbury Hill in the background, © 2004 Steve Alexander

and buried their dead. Silbury Hill, or "Cosmic Connector" has been the center of crop circle activity for decades.

As soon as we entered the Sun and Moon crop circle, it felt like a homecoming. From the moment that I saw it on the Internet a week before our departure, it was the only circle with which I felt a connection. Its special location, directly in front of West Kennett Long Barrow and across from Silbury Hill, both places I've grown to love in the past few years, made this circle especially meaningful. Walking into it through the tram, I saw that the wheat had an aura of purple. We were all immediately giddy from the impact of energy, and Jodi, Meryl, Keir, and I all lay down, putting our heads in the center of the circle like the spokes of a wheel. The sun was out, and the weather perfect. Keir had his iPod, with two headphones, and I could hear the classical music he was playing. I borrowed one of his earphones and as I lay there listening, I found myself with my arms extended in the air above me, conducting to the music. When I realized what I was doing, I turned to Jodi to show her. In that moment, I had become the conductor in this field. And perhaps—just maybe—this was the field that we would be in when the balls of light appeared to us.

A few days later, some of us were waiting by our car, parked outside our hotel in Marlborough. Jodi and I watched as three little girls in fairy costumes with magic wands chased each other outside the hotel. Knowing my vision, I asked Jodi, "Are you seeing this?" She nodded she was. "What do you think it means?" she asked me. "It means the Universe can be very confusing sometimes," I replied.

In keeping with my vision, I'd brought three magic wands from my neighborhood toy store to Wiltshire with me. As I watched the children playing, all I could think of was that I guess we didn't have to have fairy costumes and magic wands to witness something happening in the field. Here was my vision, only it wasn't us in a field, it was three little girls playing. It was confusing. Maybe nothing was going to happen after all. Divine Will is so unpredictable. Then again, perhaps this would be the night, the night three of us would stand in a field and the balls of light would grace us with their presence at last.

That night, Jodi and I had dinner with Tony, a lovely Brit who was paying a lot of attention to Jodi. After dinner we were going to meet Michael and drive back to the Sun and Moon circle for sunset. Keir and

Cam had gone to Devizes, a nearby town, to see a movie. By the time the sun had set, we had settled into the circle, cameras in hand. I had my digital 35mm around my neck, and Michael went off into the distance with his video camera and tripod. Tony, Jodi, and I formed a circle, and Jodi began to tone. The tones were rich and engulfing. I was taking pictures periodically, turning first one direction and then another.

Over the hill in the distance, two huge intensely bright disks of light appeared. Jodi was in full channel, and even though her eyes were closed, she was aware that something was going on. The sky was bright with the spheres of light, and in the distance Michael was filming them. I thought at first that the mother ship had landed. Then out from the sides of the disks of light there was a stream of smoke that looked odd to Tony and me. Tony whispered that these might be military flares. As another flare appeared in the sky, the light on the horizon seemed to ebb and flow along with Jodi's voice, as the man-made phenomena seem to be responding to Jodi's tones. At one point, I turned around and jumped in total fear when I saw a huge orange sphere hanging in the sky. Seeing my reaction, Tony reassured me that it was the moon. Both the flares and the moon served as good examples of similitude.

With the presence of the flares still in the distance, out of nowhere two balls of light appeared and danced six feet in front of the three of us. I took two shots and I knew the camera had recorded them. Then I let my camera hang around my neck, and I simply enjoyed them. In a few seconds, I realized that what the dancing balls were sending was pure love. I felt an overwhelming sense of love and choked back tears of gratitude that the experience I had sought for so long had at last occurred. Tony saw them as well, and Jodi was aware of something happening, but was too deeply in channel to open her eyes. The balls of light disappeared as magically as they had appeared originally. I had thought this was an experience of about ten seconds, but, according to my camera's log, it was over thirty seconds. They were, at long last, verisimilitude, the true appearance of the Divine. The balls of light had appeared directly adjacent to the military flares. How quirky was that? It was such a good example of similitude and verisimilitude occurring simultaneously. I find this happens with great regularity. It's as if there is yet another test we must pass in order to shift ourselves forward

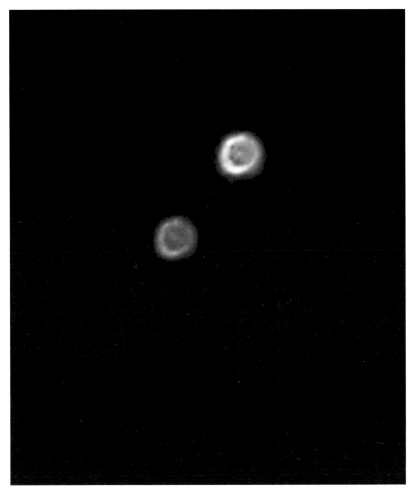

The balls of light from the Sun and Moon crop circle, © 2004

within our belief system. What is and isn't real occurs simultaneously like continuous pop quizzes from God. There is always duality. We need darkness to know light.

At that point, the flares no longer lit the sky and, once again, the night surrounded us. We began to head toward Michael, who seemed angry.

"Did you see the balls come?" I asked.

"They were about six feet from us!" Michael insisted they were flares, military flares, and that was all. But I wasn't talking about the huge bright flares in the distance. I was talking about the two balls of light that were right in front of us. Yes, Tony agreed, he'd seen them as well.

"They sent us love." I said. Although Michael had missed our experience, he had, in fact, seen a blue ball of light hanging in the distance.

Our experience had provided a good analogy for consciousness that was a lesson for all of us. What he was shooting out there over the horizon, he thought was the bigger picture, the expanded picture. It wasn't. The bigger picture, the true one, was right in front of us—closer, in the smaller frame. We have to focus inward, within the smaller frame of ourselves and our own lives, to see the bigger picture. And then when we do, when our vision expands, what we see is reflected back to us again in the smaller frame of ourselves. It's the Divine that's within each of us.

Coming back to New York City from Wiltshire was a letdown. I missed the land and the circles, and I particularly missed the balls of light. I thought, why couldn't they come here? Why don't they come and stay with me here? They could share Keir's and my home. That would be amazing. I knew of Robbert's experience in Holland, and I felt that if they could live in Robbert's house, they could live in mine as well. I could photograph them too, if they would allow it. I made a print of one of my photos of the two hovering balls of light, the one in which they had appeared closest to me and framed it. It's on one of my bedroom altars, where it sits amidst images of my family, friends, and Masters whom I love.

Derek happened to be in town for the launch party celebrating the publication of *Focus*. Jodi and I showed Derek Robbert's photos of the balls of light/beings we'd just recently seen in a crop circle in England. I suggested that perhaps Jodi and I could pay Robbert a visit in Holland, as the beings were cohabitating with him and his family. And then we all agreed that trip wasn't really necessary, as they could be here just as easily as in England or Holland.

Blue Burn

Not long ago, I fell asleep with a blue ball forming next to me, the deep iridescent blue swirling by my side. I put my hand out to embrace it. "So warm," I said out loud. And it was. When it touched my hand, it felt like an electrical charge was running all through my body. The blue light swirled again, and moved off, hanging farther up in the air, out of reach. My hand felt as if it had been burned by electricity, but I knew it was probably not as red as it felt. In fact, I woke several times during the night, thinking that my hand had been singed, even though I knew it hadn't.

This was an interesting change. Had this been a healing transmission? There had been other times when I'd interacted with the Rays, and their energy was cool. Last night, it was hot and electrical. Perhaps they run different energy when they're in healing modality. Or perhaps when they are hot, they're giving us "downloads" of information.

CHAPTER SIXTEEN

THE IRISH SWAMI

When Derek and Linda visited India in 2003, they went to look over a new orphanage that had been built to house one hundred children. It was a touching scene, filled with grateful children who were now healthy and safe, thanks to Derek's workshops, which provided all of this. The children had been making beautiful necklaces for all of us attending the workshops in gratitude for all that they had received from us. Derek could hold a necklace and tell exactly which child had made it.

When he and Linda prepared to leave the school, Derek spotted a beggar who had leprosy by the side of the road. He stood up as Derek approached him, and Derek held him in a loving, fearless embrace. He whispered to him that Christ was a shepherd, in that he was always willing to find the one sheep that was lost.

That evening, Derek told Linda that he felt he'd learned the lessons that would align them again, and there would be no more conflict between his commitment to service and to his family. He began to draw an image on a piece of paper as he spoke. "The truth lies in the middle between love and God," he explained. "Unless love is accompanied by truth, it is out of alignment with God." Now that he'd brought love back into balance, he and Linda could walk their path together, without pain and with joy—so that ultimately, it's a celebration.

Derek and Linda O'Neill, © 2006

The whole time he'd talked to her, he was drawing a diagram about their family and their love for each other. At the end of Derek's story, the diagram transformed into a champagne glass with bubbles that he added to represent joy and celebration. Linda and Derek had already decided to dissolve their marriage, feeling that their vows had been based on improper foundations. The next day, they would exchange marriage vows from a new understanding of truth and love. And that same day in late 2003, Derek, the psychotherapist from Dublin, was initiated as a Kriya Yoga Master and Swami.

Derek and Linda are a good model for a relationship in which two people walk side by side in support of, but not in the way of, each other. Yet, it's touching when I hear him say that he's nothing without her. Linda began doing powerful relationship workshops in the United States in 2005. She often resembles the Ascended Master Lady Nada, who represents total surrender, and whose Christed energy she also seems to embody. I took a few pictures of Linda and Derek as they stood together in Ireland last summer. Suddenly Derek held her closer and gave her a really sensual, quite lengthy kiss. And Derek, in a hand gesture waved at my camera, jammed it completely, leaving me unable to capture that moment.

"That's a good trick isn't it, Burson?" he said, "Did you like that trick?"

I laughed really hard and called him a Swami/Leprechaun once again.

Awakenings

While I was meditating recently, I saw an image of myself—or at least it felt like it was me—washing Christ's body. It was such a realistic vision. I was standing on his left side, washing his left leg and foot, while a few men were lifting him up by his arms and chest. Many others were also there attending to his body. I had no clue what to make of this one. Was I there? Was I one of the people actually there washing Christ's feet? I didn't know what to think. After sitting with such a vivid impression in my mind, I decided to e-mail Derek.

He answered, "All of those who have come to the Ireland workshops are having the same images. This is because I am awakening to you the DNA of all the people in the world, both past and present. Jesus is part of the Oversouls who are Avatars, so he can be Krishna or Buddha or whoever he wants, for he is. Christ is a consciousness, not a being. It is time for all of us to be awakened to the oneness of who we are. Each of us is everyone. There is no separation."

Derek spent the night in my loft early in 2004 on one of his trips to New York. The publication of my book *Focus* had been postponed, and I felt it was so that I could include him along with two photos in the book. He ran into Michael briefly, as he was pretty much living with me at the time. After he left, Derek gave me the best relationship advice that I've ever received. "Ask yourself, on a scale of one to ten, what is the amount of self-love you have? How would you rate that? If you're with someone who's at a six and you're a seven, it's not an even match. One person is going to keep pulling the other down, while the other is trying to pull the other person up. They'd always wonder how you could possibly love them more than they love themselves, and they'd never trust you."

We can only have trust in ourselves and in our relationship to the Divine. Placing any relationship over that, giving it more importance than our love of our God selves and the Universe is destined to be off course. It is only walking side by side without holding onto one's partner that's appropriate. It's about each of us making our own way toward God.

That night, Derek showed me the photos that were taken of him at his Swami ceremony in India. I didn't recognize Derek in the photos. He appeared to be twenty years younger, with the black hair of his youth. I asked if he had learned shape-shifting from Sai Baba, but Derek assured me that he's been shape-shifting from the age of five. It came in very handy when his mother was trying to find him! According to Derek's close friend Kieran, Derek the prankster loved to play with this one. Kieran never knows when the young Derek will suddenly show up. We talked a lot about shape-shifting that night. When Derek told me he could shift into anything, a woman or a dog, for example, I had to ask what happened to his clothes when he shapeshifted. Come to think of it, I'd never understood that about Superman either! He told me that it was really about changing molecular structure. So a wall could change into a chair. I suspected that Derek had awakened to the Avatar inherent within him.

Derek slept in my bedroom that night, and I slept in the sleeping alcove which functions as the makeshift guest room in the center of my loft. He tricked me into sleeping in the alcove. I had not intended to give up my bedroom. All of a sudden there was Derek walking into my room with his briefcase and closing the door and saying good night!

I didn't realize until six months later that the night Derek spent in my home, he opened a tremendous vortex of love in my bedroom that doesn't allow anything less than that amount of integrity to be present. Obviously, he had a plan as well as a reason to sleep in my room, although I certainly didn't realize what it was at the time. The vortex he created was like shining a beam of the brightest light imaginable to expand here in this space within my home. It is my lighthouse of truth. That light is the golden energy of Christ-consciousness, and it is the purest vibration of love. It is not a reference to an individual—it is an energy that appears as gold light. Even now, when the brilliance of direct sunlight passes through my bedroom, I can glimpse the golden-yellow grid of pure Christ-consciousness Derek placed here. I see the pattern woven into the ceiling.

There was an extra-large men's watch I'd received as a gift, which I'd placed in my bathroom in lieu of a clock. It had a voice activator in it that spoke the time. I gave it to Derek the next morning because he thought it would make a great gift for a blind person.

In the summer of 2005, I went to the Lower Manhattan Cultural Council's new offices for a meeting. Seeing as they now had a new home, I took a few minutes to houseclean their space etherically, giving them an energetic fresh start. The hustle of the office had spun my head a bit, and when I finished, I wondered if I had made an impact and lightened their space. As I got on the subway to return home, there was a dark-skinned woman in a business suit who started singing in full voice right across from where I was seated. "May Holy Spirit come down in this place," she sang out. I looked around and no one seemed to be hearing her song but me. She wouldn't look directly at me, but instead, kept singing the same line over and over in what was such a melodic refrain that I can still hear it. Waves of energy went through me, and I felt as if I'd just received validation for cleaning house at the LMCC. I thanked her as I left the subway, which also went unacknowledged. I believe she was a manifestation of Sai Baba in a knowing acknowledgment of my contribution in healing downtown. Or perhaps it was Derek as these days it is hard to tell who's who, and certainly Derek won't tell.

Are people with the power to heal or change themselves into other people more God than we are? Just because they are more powerful than we are, doesn't mean that we should turn our power over to them. Any teacher who asks that of us is questionable. They are here to teach us to be our own Gurus. When children at Derek's orphanages throw rose petals at him, he throws them back.

Over three thousand children to date are either living in Derek's orphanages or are going through the orphanages he has sponsored. His sponsorship has built a primary school and secondary school that are both in the Tamil Nadu and Bangalore areas of India. The children are given accommodations until they are educated enough to get jobs. Those choosing to go to college will be able to go to the one that's just been built. The first part opened on Sai Baba's birthday in November 2005, and the second section opened on Derek's birthday in June 2006.

The Born Free Now Foundation built and runs the new Tiruvannamalai Animal Rescue Center in India. Derek's humanitarian efforts have now spread to two continents, addressing the foundation's ultimate goal of worldwide outreach to impoverished children everywhere. These projects include a new school in El Salvador for the children who live in a remote mountain sector and an indigenous health and education project in the Peruvian Amazon.

The Creacon Lodge Prema Agni Healing Center, which opened in February 2007, has been described as the most powerful vortex ever experienced. Located in the gorgeous country setting of Wexford, Ireland, visitors say it is like being wrapped in a blanket of Love. There is a rainbow bridge connecting the heart of Derek's new center to the heart of Sai Baba's ashram in Puttaparthi, India.

After my friend and powerful healer MJ Sawyer and I left one of Derek's workshops, we were so high it took us an hour to find the subway. Being high on energy is the best possible drug. In Derek's presence, I have been able to pour more light into my body than ever before. He carries more Christed gold energy, the energy of pure Love, than I have experienced from anyone in a human body, although I have not, as yet, visited India. I believe he is an Avatar, perhaps even a Purna, or complete Avatar. Through his presence, I have accessed breathtaking multi-dimensional portals so profound that they were life-changing. I've even experienced a full-blown Kriyatic state in his workshops. It's a state sometimes referred to by healers as the "flopping fish" phenomenon!

I wanted to make some photos using Derek's Vibhuti (sacred healing ash), and my friend MJ volunteered to help. My idea was to use the 20 x 24-inch large format Polaroid camera (there are only four of these in the world, and, luckily, one is right down the street from me) and pour the Vibhuti into the frame of the big Polaroid. It would appear to fall the same way as when Sai Baba manifests it from his hands. Derek, however, usually manifests it differently from Sai Baba. Derek makes it by shaking up the box of Vibhuti that Sai Baba gave him. When he does, the Vibhuti in the box keeps multiplying, so there is always as much as he needs. When Derek brought me the Vibhuti for the shoot, I put it in a small Tupperware container. It expanded, and I put it in a much bigger Tupperware container. By the day of the shoot, it was half full, and as MJ and I began to pour it for the photos, it kept expanding. It was a magical day, blessed by the Swami/Leprechaun, and the other Masters, too. In fact, a few weeks before the shoot, I was sitting with a friend at my computer looking at a few e-mails we were discussing. Suddenly, out of nowhere, a short video of Sai Baba manifesting Vibhuti appeared on my computer screen and lasted for about five seconds. It was particularly amazing seeing it because the Internet hadn't even been on, and yet, there was Sai Baba, with Vibhuti pouring from his hand! It felt as if he also had given his personal Blessing for my pictures.

A few years ago, Derek gave his tin of Vibhuti to someone he felt needed an awakening. Six months later, the man returned it to him, saying that it didn't produce Vibhuti, and it was only a tin. Derek told him that chasing the tin was like seeking the Holy Grail, which was, after all, only a wooden cup. "It's the energy of the tin that's important," he told him. Derek put his hand over the tin and it was immediately filled.

In 2003, Derek had also begun to manifest jewelry in his hands as gifts. Manifesting jewelry in his hands was a new trick I hadn't seen Derek do before, and I knew for sure he was meeting privately with Sai Baba, because manifesting jewelry is one of the things Sai Baba is famous for. He manifests "things" for people, because he feels that objects are good tools for people to maintain a focus. In fact, the pendant that Derek manifested for me has a photo of Satya Sai Baba on one side and Shirdi Sai Baba (the first incarnation of Sai Baba) on the other. That pendant is what I most appreciate having around me when I meditate.

Sondra Shaye, Derek's agent, was once leaving a Starbuck's in Brooklyn, having just bought a cup of Derek's favorite hot chocolate. A homeless man approached her and asked for a sip of her chocolate. Sondra responded with a five-dollar bill that she took out of her purse and handed to him. When she got home there was an e-mail from Derek in Dublin, which said, "I didn't ask you for money, I asked you for some of your hot chocolate!"

During a lunch break at Derek's Santa Monica workshop a few years back, I saw a dollar bill come floating down in front of me in the middle of Santa Monica Boulevard. I picked it up and asked my friends whom it belonged to. I was told it probably belonged to the homeless man who was sitting down the street outside the hotel. I put it in my wallet and said I'd give it back to him when we returned after lunch.

When we left the restaurant, I took the dollar out and added another ten-dollar bill to it, making it (the magic number) eleven dollars. As I placed it in the beggar's cup, he said, "Thank you!" and I looked into his very blue eyes and said, "You're welcome." I knew when I saw his eyes there was the presence of God inside this man. I recognized those eyes and that energy, and they both seemed like Derek's! A huge wave of energy went through me as I smiled and walked away. We arrived back at the workshop, where all of us had begun to assemble, preparing ourselves for the afternoon's meditations. When Derek came in, the first thing he said was, "Eleven dollars would have been just the right amount to give that homeless man in front of the hotel." When Derek and I talked about that incident months later, he wouldn't reveal whether that incident had been "overshadowing," the term he uses to describe taking on someone else's body, or shape-shifting.

Derek's aura is extremely rare. It has been described as a Mobius strip, or sideways figure eight, that cuts across his solar plexus, forming a cross. He has studied within the Hindu tradition, but is very much a part of the lineage of Christ-consciousness. I believe Derek O'Neill is a part of Christ's soul group; he is an Ascended Master in human form and part of the lineage of masters such as Krishna, Buddha, Mohammed, and Jesus. Derek is here to serve planet Earth as mass consciousness evolves. When the students are ready, the teachers arrive. And when Derek asks us to give him our pain or fear, he means it.

According to Derek, before Jesus' crucifixion, the Council of Ein Soph headed by the Ascended Master Melchizedek met to discuss how Jesus of Nazareth would endure his ordeal. They had agreed he'd be flogged as a way of preparing him for crucifixion, with the understanding that he would utilize all his Yogic powers to withstand his pain. The point at which the council removed his Yogic powers was the moment that Jesus said "Father, why have you forsaken me?" Then the Council laid into him the Prema Agni symbol as well as the Rising Star (the symbol that represents the healing system that the Masters brought to us through Derek) and with the vibration of these two symbols, he rose to be the great Way-Shower, whereas before he was simply Jesus of Nazareth.

It is apparent in a way that I have just begun to understand that the Rays are here to assist in writing this book. Previously, I had not considered myself a direct channel in the same manner as other friends of mine, but now I'm beginning to discover that information conveyed to me is coming in faster and more easily.

I have not been allowed to take pictures of Mary or the Rays. I am, however, supposed to show the Rays to others and have been told that photos will come after the beginning of 2006, in keeping with what seems to be Divine timing. One evening, I sat in the dark with my camera and asked again, just to make sure I'd heard them correctly. I discovered it's best to call a meeting with the Rays before my bedtime to discuss what I consider to be the serious issues. It helps me clearly discern their communications.

Each of us hears a particular tone that we recognize as our own voice when we think inside our heads. If we think about what that inner voice sounds like, it becomes easier to access our guidance. The Rays speak in a tone that's a little quieter and a little more formal than my own inner voice. It's also a good way to recognize that these are not just our own thoughts, but our guides speaking to us. In communicating with the Rays, we will likely be "hearing" them and taking in messages in our own voices, as they don't have voice boxes, but usually communicate intuitively.

Orbs: Intend them, and they will come.
August 21, 2005

Over the past few years, I've seen a lot of digital images that have been sent to me through the Internet. One large orb appearing in the middle of a photo is probably an artifact and not an actual orb. Sometimes a lens flare will produce similitude as well. Although one could argue the point by saying that everything comes from God, it still interests me to discern what is similitude and what is verisimilitude. Orbs are likely to show up at festive occasions or whenever there is group intention, as with meditation or prayer. They even seem to have the ability to visually reflect our thoughts back to us by physically manifesting the faces of deceased loved ones within them. Seventy billion digital images will be taken this year alone—a plethora of real orbs are just waiting to be captured. Intend them, and you will be amazed at the results.

I believe that the orbs are here as the first rung on the ladder of energies with which humans are meant to interact. The Rays constitute the second, as both act as portals to conscious awareness. In my experience, orbs listen, and Rays, or Light Beings talk. And the orbs don't share their luminosity with humans as the Rays do.

In January 2007, the Rays gave me more information about the orbs. "Orbs are like the cells that float around our bodies. They are the cells of the Universe. They are like small bits of consciousness that float in the cosmic soup of what constitutes all time and space. Sometimes within a spherical structure there is an entire being and sometimes it's just a cell that's conscious. All float within the causal sea of intention. Orbs are here to teach us that everything in the Universe has consciousness, so the power of intention will manifest their appearance. When you intend them, you pull them towards you in an energetic embrace between man and God. The mist (which appears as millions of tiny orbs clumped together) is the Universe's ectoplasm and a reminder that we are all connected. Like the orbs, the mist is governed by the Law of Attraction, so it follows the positive energies, coming along for the joy and fun of being in the energy of Love."

A Ray over the net in a photo that Nancy calls *The Divine Setup*, © 2003

CHAPTER SEVENTEEN

HELP THE HEALERS HEAL

Sri Swami Yukteswar had appeared to me initially in 1998, and I hadn't seen anything of him since. He lived in India from 1855 to 1936. One book of his teachings titled *The Holy Science* was written by him, and *Autobiography of a Yogi* by Paramahamsa Yogananda was written about him. On his initial visit to me, I saw him quite distinctly in what I would call the first real vision I'd ever had. According to Derek, he had been sent by Sai Baba to give me my "assignment." That assignment was to "help the healers heal." In response I said to him, "Oh, great. What about me?"

And he said, "You are well. Eat anything you like." When he dissolved, I was left with the feeling that the Universe had truly opened to me in a way I'd not considered possible, and all I did in return was complain. I've always wished that I'd expressed at least some gratitude to him.

In September 2005, I saw him sitting at a little round table watching me. I think he might have even smiled at me—or at least I would have wanted a smile from him, as a student wants approval from the teacher. In any case, it made me happy to see Sri Yukteswar—my Master on the other side. It was Derek who revealed exactly who had given me my assignment. Once I understood that my mission was to help the healers heal, I began to delve into all aspects of what that statement could mean, eventually covering all the possibilities. First, I could help the healers heal by introducing them to members of the medical community who, after seeing convincing demonstrations of energetic healing, would understand that healing can be as acceptable as any form of acupuncture or homeopathy. This, in turn, would lead to its acceptance as a useful tool in standard medical practice. This is the way it is in England, where healers meet stringent requirements and only qualify as such through successful case histories that are well-

Sri Yukteswar

documented. The collaboration of doctors and healers is more accepted and far more common than here in the United States.

Another interpretation was "help the healers themselves to be healed." No doubt over the years, my grounded-ness has been appreciated by my friends, accompanied with the give and take that is the appropriate earmark of good friendship. Every one of us in a human body needs periodic guidance, and, certainly, my dearest friends, no matter how powerful, are no exception. Artists make what they need to see, writers write what they need to know, and healers heal what they need to have healed in themselves. And look at all I've received in return! How privileged I am to have such close relationships with those who have taught me lifetimes of knowledge in this one. And in the bigger picture, "help the healers to heal" is also a reference to the thousands of light workers worldwide who are focusing intention for a more peaceful planet on a daily and nightly basis. As more and more of us step into our Mastery, my job continues as friends around the globe align to become an even greater force of Light on this Earth.

Over the years, I have wondered whether I'd ever see Sri Yukteswar again and what he'd have to say to me when we did meet. And would I be more gracious in his presence than I was the first time? One summer, when I was in Ireland along with eighty others attending Derek's workshop, the Irish Swami handed me the Yukteswar book, *The Holy Science*. It's a comparison between Christianity and Hinduism. Obviously, he is the appropriate Divine teacher to guide me along my path, as my focus now is to assist in bringing all faiths together into the one true religion, which is Love. A few years ago, Keir gave me two head-bobbing figures, one of Jesus, and one of the Indian God Shiva. They stand facing each other in our kitchen, ever-present symbols of the dialogue that inspires me. When Derek handed me the book, he told me that Sri Swami Yukteswar would prefer I refer to his hair as silver instead of gray, as I'd originally described it in *Focus*. Now does he really care how I refer to his hair color? He is, after all, an Ascended Master and above ego. Is Derek teasing me a bit, being the leprechaun that he is? Or am I just supposed to be aware of the irony of what he's just said and be doubled up on the floor laughing?

CHAPTER EIGHTEEN

LOVE BUGS

August 22, 2005

The beings don't usually appear in full form, but as blue balls of light, which they know are less intimidating than their little faces. They tease me. I woke up once to an image of a nondescript black bug. I felt the image come from my right side where my usual guy appears next to me. The bug image wasn't visually clear to me. It was more of an impression. A minute later, it was replaced by an image of a grasshopper. Now that was a clear message and was quite funny! Just in case I'd forgotten that every thought is heard! Grasshopper-face was what he was calling himself, his way of jokingly announcing himself and also a reference to my telling them their faces resemble insects. "Okay," I said, "but do you have to wake me up to tell me a joke? Couldn't it have waited until morning? I already know how funny you can be." Then I heard, "Love Bugs, love from the bugs. We are the Love Bugs." How funny and poignant they are, and how many levels of wordplay they utilize. Love from the bugs, as well as the Love Bugs! How privileged I am to be part of this new level of loving communion with the Universe, and to have the guidance of those who have been here practicing love since the beginning of time.

Conscious Communication

I once thought that metaphysics was simply the study of being and knowing. What I heard during meditation is that the way to lead is with our hearts and not with our heads. Consciousness is a commitment to fully recognizing who we are and having the willingness to see that daily until we die. And then we can come back and do it all over again. It is also a commitment to fully love everyone, starting with ourselves, without judgment. How do our religions serve us if we continue to worship God from the point of view of separation? As long as we continue to fight over God, our judgments will create wars in God's name. If we insist on our religious differences, the least we can do is be tolerant of our neighbor's beliefs.

Blue is the color of the throat chakra, through which we all communicate. Therefore when teaching or speaking, it is helpful to intend a megaphone of blue energy emanating from our throats. Spirit seen in the form of blue patches of energy represents Divine communication to me. More specifically, it is blue that is associated with the energy of Mother Mary and Quan Yin, as well as the Archangel Gabriel.

One night as I watched Mary dance and waited for the Love Bugs to appear, I was greeted by a red sphere emanating from Mary, instead of blue.

I had seen this red energy for about a week, and it startled me when I did. It's confusing to me since I had never seen much of the red spectrum before, except on Jodi's lawn, and I didn't get what it was doing here now. I know red auras are unresolved anger issues, so I'm not so sure that when I'm seeing this red energy, it's from the highest vibration of love and here for my highest good. When I saw red emanating from Mary, I said, "You know I really like it better when you're blue." Immediately I saw purple balls, the combination of red and blue together. This is, after all, collaboration, and a continuing dialogue between my hue-man self and the Universe. It's a relationship that's a blending of colors, of dimensions, and of peaceful co-existence on all levels. It's the promise that the future can be better than the present if we let go of our differences and judgments.

Change of Color
September 9, 2005

I haven't seen much of the Rays—or at least I'm not seeing them as visibly—or as blue as before. In the darkness around my bed each night I see more luminosity and opaque whiteness than blue. Since I'm aware that they know I'm wary of their "redness" when they show up as that color, I decided to literally take the matter into my own hand. I held out my hand to where I saw a faint luminosity hovering beside me. As I held it in my hand, I asked it out loud whether it could turn red. Immediately, I was holding a red ball of energy in my hand.

April/May 2007

The Rays have revealed more about the red energy around them. "Red is the energy that propels forward, like a jet stream or a motor. Hot and cool, hot and cool. It's the Universe's equilibrium, holding the balance. For propulsion of more energy, additional red is required." Therefore, more red is visible as the Rays utilize more energy to appear in this dimension of humans and their cameras. The red energy is their jet propulsion system.

Recent photos reveal that the red energies manifest in an enormous range of sizes. In some images, the red energy is quite small, appearing like a tiny rudder skirting the edges of the Blue Rays. Yet other images from presentations reveal huge streaks of red in the sky similar to the ones I originally saw on Jodi's lawn upstate.

CHAPTER NINETEEN

BALLS OF LIGHT

In the early 80s, Isabelle was asked by Spirit to go back to Wiltshire, where she had been born. She had been instructed to walk the land, nurturing it with light and intention. Accompanied by a group of about twenty locals from all walks of life in Wiltshire, they walked the land in all the seasons and in all kinds of weather. They trusted Isabelle's vision that this is what God required of them. They walked the land for four years, without really knowing why.

Isabelle's job was to serve as the link between the "Watchers," the name of a collective intelligence guiding humans that came to Isabelle through Merlin, and the group of light workers who still assist her in adding conscious intention to the land. The Watchers asked her to help open the sacred sites to receive light, setting up the appropriate vibration to communicate with us and illuminating the path to consciousness. What would happen next was unknown to everyone, including Isabelle. Then, in the mid 80s, Isabelle received another message: "It will be as if the hand of God has touched the land." And then, "Within the week, you will get a sign. You will see; there will be a sign."

Isabelle spent that week outside, waiting. She paced, prayed, and waited. Nothing. After several days, she was exhausted. She had no idea what she was waiting for. A spaceship? An angel?

On the last night, Isabelle was once again outside the house waiting for something to happen. She lay down in the grass in the garden and fell asleep until the ringing phone woke her.

"You'll never guess what happened," her friend told her with great excitement. "I was driving home this evening and an orange ball of light followed my car all the way home. It was incredible! What do you think it meant?" the friend asked Isabelle.

Isabelle's nose was a little out of joint because her friend got the "sign" she'd been waiting for. And yet she understood that this is exactly the way the Universe works. It was a good lesson in detaching from her ego regarding her relationship to Spirit. She realized these gifts from Source aren't really just about us. They're about the consciousness of all things, all people.

Isabelle awoke the next morning to an image of a circle drawn into the land. It was what some called a "Fairy Ring." At last she knew that this is what Merlin meant. Somewhere on the land nearby was a circle or two embedded in a field. A friend from her group who'd been walking the land with her all those years stopped by. Excited and out of breath, Isabelle knew what her friend was going to say. She'd already seen it psychically.

"It's a fairy circle, isn't it?" Isabelle suggested.

"Yes," her friend told her. Together they went to examine the field, and there before them lay many circles in a field of wheat across from Silbury Hill, glistening brilliantly in the sunlight.

Spending a few days with Isabelle and the crop circles were seductive for Keir and me. After all, we live in New York City. Sitting in a circular vortex of wheat is both grounding and healing. We were overjoyed to simply spend time in the glyphs. The fields themselves would sometimes display a purple aura, and most visits were accompanied by the giggling and giddiness that is the hallmark of the crop circle experience.

The Watchers, Isabelle explained to us as we sat in one of the circles, are here to help humanity choose. Will we be responsible to ourselves and to our Earth, or will we muck it up? Only we can decide. If they came to all of us in physical form, it would be a decision made outside of ourselves, a decision made for us. Protecting people from experience doesn't lead to real understanding. We must each develop our God selves and understand that we're all a part of the big picture. The circles, Isabelle told us, are here for us as messages to receive the conscious awareness that we are responsible for our reality, in that we weave what we create. That each of us interprets them and feels them differently is totally appropriate, since no two of us are alike, even though we are all connected.

"Bottom line," Isabelle told us, smiling, "is this: It is said that highly evolved beings are known by their sense of humor." She went on to say that in the late 80s, Merlin told her, "We will give you the key." And Isabelle thought, "At last we'll have all the information we need." Two days later, the first crop circle in the shape of a key, appeared on the land.

An army helicopter flew overhead, which led us to the question: What is the government's role here? Are they simply as curious as the rest of us, or do they have a role in keeping actual scientific evidence of the circles a secret? They are continuing to receive bad press on both sides of the Atlantic. Prince Charles planned a visit here and had to cancel his trip because of the controversy that even a proposed visit caused. In fact, these days, crop circles are even a joke, a bad joke, on *Saturday Night Live* (2005). In a scathing documentary produced in 2004 by *Scientific American*, once again the entire phenomenon was discounted, and the BLT (BLT Research Team, Inc.) group unfairly discredited.

In the summer of 2005, a friend of mine watched a game of cat-and-mouse between a ball of light and a military helicopter over a crop circle in Savernake Forest, outside of Marlborough. In my opinion, most humans don't understand the messages from the crop circles. Those messages, the real ones, are lost in the controversy over who made them. If teams of hoaxers made all the crop circles, as many hoaxers have in Wiltshire over the past few years, how could they be in so many places in the world simultaneously? They have even been documented as forming in daylight, such as the case with the first Julia Set formation, which appeared beside Stonehenge one morning in 1996.

At least here in the States, it is acceptable to say that some of the circles are man-made and some are not. That alone is a huge step forward.

Thousands of circles have landed not only in wheat, barley, and rapeseed, but in sand and ice. As of 2005 over 10,000 have appeared in twenty-nine countries. They have been seen everywhere, from Africa to Greenland, across Europe, through the Middle East, Canada, and the United States. Historical indications show crop circles are not new. There is a documented report by a scientist in Britain in 1686, with drawings and an explanation of the phenomena. In July 1880, an article appeared in the prestigious science journal *Nature*, which described a circle. Photos of circles in England dating from the early 1900s also exist.

With the land in England composed of limestone and chalk, and the sacred sites that line up with the energies of the ley lines, eighty percent of the world's crop circles fall there in the summer. As I consider myself to be an investigative photographer, I have developed relationships with many whom I consider to be the most prominent researchers in the study of the circles. I know Nancy Talbot and John Burke, both of BLT Research Team, Inc., and I know they are people of integrity. After years of study, their basic findings include the following: There are differences between the electromagnetic charges inside and outside of the circles. Some of the nodes of the wheat are "blown" by the intense microwave heat that seems to be hitting the fields for only a few seconds. Semi-molten particles consistent with the descending plasma vortices have also been found. In the places where the circles are formed, the wheat is permanently affected and has been found to be taller and heartier than the wheat surrounding it, and it stays that way year after year.

The Blend of Colors
September 13, 2005
The balls of light gathered around me in their nighttime ritual but appeared in purple this time. I watched as they shifted and turned to green with flickering yellow sparkles in the mix. I lay there thinking that they're tangibly showing me they can become any color. So perhaps all I have to do is ask for whatever color I want. If they honor my request to change color, it would make sense that I could probably demonstrate this shift to others. It would be a few levels up from show-

ing people how to see aura, which I've been demonstrating for many years now. Mary, then, would be the instrument, the vehicle for people to arrive at their own truth.

Consciousness comes in all colors, all shapes, and all sizes and is represented in every shape and form on the planet. It's a simple message, without confusion. It doesn't matter who we are or where we come from. We're the same, even though we are unique.

CHAPTER TWENTY

THE WAY HOME

In 2005 there was no way Jodi would leave her new META Center in New York City for the annual trip to Wiltshire. I understood it as a test of my own relationship with the Universe. I could do this work myself. I didn't need anyone to help me. All I had to do was ask God to help and he/she/it would comply.

Before the trip, I mailed letters to myself and several other people with my pre-visions of Wiltshire 2005. A part of it read: "On Monday, July 11, I awoke to a vision in which my friend Bearcloud and I were on top of Silbury Hill at night. We watched, and I think we filmed something as well. I felt like we were turning from facing the front of Silbury Hill, the side by the highway. It felt like we saw a circle being made."

Meryl and I arrived the morning of July 25, and that night, Bearcloud and I did go up Silbury Hill. I took my video camera and did some filming, as I was expecting something to happen while we were there. I kept my camera focused southwest, the direction of West Kennett Long Barrow. I sat in the darkness, camera poised, while Bearcloud slept. What I didn't realize was that the circle I thought would be created that night had already fallen the night before, when Meryl and I were flying in. Because of the bad weather, it hadn't as yet been documented from the air. It appeared one field over from where the Sun and Moon circle was the previous summer, and both West Kennett Long Barrow and Silbury Hill were visible from a distance.

When Meryl and I went there the next day, we discovered a relatively small formation shaped like a cake cut into twelve slices. We'd run into a group of healers from the Southwest, and since there were twelve of us, someone decided that it would make a good picture if we all put our heads in the center. It was easier said that done, because as soon as we formed a circle someone in the group would stand up to take a picture. It was hilarious chaos. Finally I explained that I was a professional and would be glad to take pictures and e-mail them to whomever.

The man lying next to me gave me his card, which read "Focus on Peace." I could hardly believe what I was seeing. Focus on Peace was the name of the project I did with the Lower Manhattan Cultural Council for the first anniversary of 9/11. It consisted of 7,000 posters and 30,000 postcards that were distributed around the WTC site for that first anniversary. Receiving that card felt to me like acknowledge-

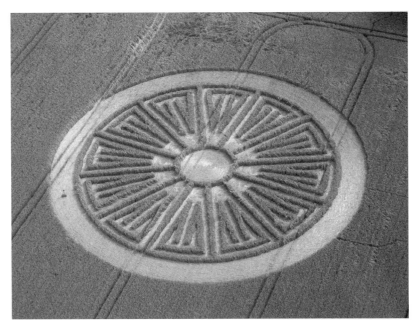

Pie crop circle, © 2005

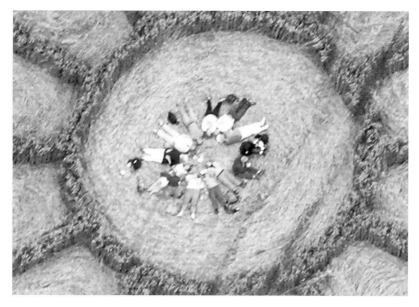

Inside the Pie crop circle at the exact moment Nancy (sitting up in black) receives "Focus on Peace" card, © 2005 Stuart Dike

ment of my vision, and it was a reminder that there are no accidents or coincidences. The Universe is always fully in charge of the sacred plan. At that point, God in the form of a plane flew over us shooting photos that were published on the Internet, and that are now in the archives of the Crop Circle Connector website. In that aerial photo, that man and I were the only two people sitting up in the circle. The plane had documented him handing me his card that said, "Focus on Peace."

From inside the Pie crop circle, Meryl noticed that a pattern appeared in the sky. I saw it as well. It looked like a huge world grid that crisscrossed in a delicate purplish pattern across the sky. It was as if a giant cosmic spider had woven us into its web and connected us with all that there is.

18/75

When Meryl and I arrived in Marlborough that year, my first question to Isabelle was, "What is Smeathe's Ridge?" Its coordinates, I told her, were the first information I'd received from the Rays a few weeks before. She replied that Smeathe's Ridge is the Sirian vortex that she and her group had opened on the land in the late 90s. The information had surprised me. I thought this would be the place that the Universal consciousness would place a crop circle and that they had given me advanced knowledge of it by sending me the exact coordinates for where the circle would land. I had mailed several letters to colleagues and to myself with the pre-cognitive information about what I thought would happen during the summer in Wiltshire, 2005. So Isabelle's information that Smeathe's Ridge was a vortex wasn't at all what I'd expected. I was expecting a crop circle to land there. After all, there were wheat fields on either side. And I had been shown a circle being made before I'd left for Wiltshire, which I'd also mentioned in the letter of pre-visions I'd written.

Between the bouts of nasty weather our first week, Meryl, Pete, our driver, and I went to investigate Smeathe's Ridge. Young Pete Hemery grew up on metaphysics. His parents are David and V. Hemery. David is one of Isabelle's colleagues, an author, and former Olympic champion, and V. is a top homeopath. Both are students and friends of Isabelle

View from the tumali atop Smeathe's Ridge, Wiltshire, England, © 2005

and have walked the land with her for many years. It is not an easy hike, but it is an historic one. The road through the woods and fields and out onto the ridgeway itself is the oldest road in England, dating back thousands of years. The grass has grown on top of most of the old stones that peek from beneath the tall grass. Farmlands and wheat fields are on either side of the ridgeway, and a small clump of trees down below is called Smeathe's Plantation. Further off in the distance is Four Mile Clump, another group of trees. (Unlike Americans, the English name every topographical nuance on their ancient land.) A tumali, or burial mound, sits at the highest spot, dotted with wildflowers.

In another part of the letter of my pre-visions of Wiltshire, I wrote, "I've heard a verse to a song called 'The Prayer' by Celine Dion several times now. The verse goes . . . 'Lead us to a place, Guide us with your Grace, to a place where we'll be safe.' When I heard this song, I saw myself walking in a field with several other people, and I was pointing something out to them. I think it was the daytime."

Keetsoff and Moran were the words I had heard and written down before we left that morning. It sounded like a name to me. I knew these words were important, and I couldn't figure out what they meant. As the three of us walked out onto the ridgeway for the first time, we crossed the fields, hiked up the steep hills and over a barbed wire fence. We learned to dodge the patches of stinging nettle, and Pete found us dock leaves, the antidote to relieve the burning of the nettles. I acknowledged him as our guide to this magical place and recognized the land from the vision that I had of us going there, as we hiked along trusting Pete's intuition of the local terrain. Standing on the top of the tumali, looking down at the fields on both sides below, Smeathe's Ridge is both a windy and enchanting place. Isabelle often walks along the path adjacent to the fields, as it's only a few miles from her house. Sitting on top of the tumali, I felt like I could never get enough of this place. It was somehow a part of my heart, probably a remnant of a time past.

Since I so clearly felt that there would be a crop circle on one side or another there, I asked our dear accommodating Pete to bring me back. He and his friend Erin joined me that night, and we arranged to hike out there before sunset, making it easier to see our way out onto the ridge. We stayed a few very cold hours in the wind and the light rain and left about midnight. I was disappointed not to spend the whole night but saw that it wasn't a viable alternative. We'd brought one sleeping bag, which wasn't going to fit all three of us.

The next day, Meryl, Isabelle, and I again went up to the ridge, and, together, we set an intention for a circle to appear there, if not that summer, then the next. A few days later, Pete, Bearcloud, and I went back to Smeathe's Ridge. On the way back, the two of them walked ahead of me, as I lingered not wanting to leave. I found myself suddenly overwhelmed with emotion, and tears poured from me and evaporated quickly in the wind. I wept without understanding why, and then I heard, "It's the home of your soul." When I heard that, I couldn't help but wonder whether I'd been the person buried underneath the tumali that adorns the top of Smeathe's Ridge. Soul is a word used so often, yet not a word often used by me. Maybe because the catch phrase "soul-mate" always threw me conceptually as I found it so overused, or maybe because the soul is such a vast concept and seldom understood.

Many years ago, I awoke to the presence of an egg-shaped light form hovering a few feet above me. The pink, silver, and gold specks of light within the egg shimmered and then dissipated. I heard my guidance tell me it was my soul. We'd been working on healing our souls in night school and unhealed wounds energetically appear as cracks and tatters in the eggshell. An unwillingness to forgive, for example, will manifest as a crack in the shell indicating where we're in separation from God.

But if Smeathe's Ridge is really a Sirian portal, then clearly it isn't the home of just my soul, but the home of all our souls. Of course, that had to be it! No wonder I was so at home here. I was grateful for both the answer and for the reason it was so hard for me to leave.

According to Isabelle, the ancient people superimposed mirror images of the constellations on the landscape. It's as if they looked to the heavens and made a copy for themselves on the land. Canis Major is the constellation that was the heavenly mirror for the land in Wiltshire, and Sirius is a star within that constellation.

When I returned to New York, I told Keir all about Smeathe's Ridge, as I only mentioned it briefly when we'd spoken by phone. He'd needed a year off from Wiltshire that year, he told me, but would certainly return in 2006. When we compared notes about that particular day and time that the Ridge was revealed as my soul's home, Keir was eating lunch at his favorite restaurant. And in that same moment, with an ocean between us, he'd decided that for some reason he would have to move to Wiltshire for a few years, as the land had suddenly called to him.

The day before I left for New York, dearest Pete and I returned for the fifth and final time to Smeathe's Ridge that year. We took offerings of Poland Spring water I'd brought with me from New York and some small crystals that I buried in the ground at the top of the tumali in a heartfelt ceremony of gratitude and love for that place. And leaving, once again, I had the same emotional outpouring, pulling myself together only to get over the barbed wire fence that was a continuing challenge.

I discovered some little rubber figures at the toy store in Marlborough to take home as gifts. There's a smiling yellow human and a blue-being guy. I would probably call him an alien guy if I didn't know ETs would prefer to be called beings, as we all are. When I returned from England, I placed both on my bedroom altar, arranging them so they're holding hands. They were my silly little gifts for Jodi, but it's hard to surprise a psychic! "You're bringing me back two little figures," she said!

Later that day, I met Isabelle for an early dinner and to say goodbye until next year. I asked her where the beings are from exactly. Are they Sirians or Pleideans or Archturians? Are they tall or short? She said to think of it as how it is on Earth. Some of us are dark-skinned and some light, some tall and some short. It really doesn't matter, as it's a collective. They're all part of the Universal family, and there is no separation.

We talked about Smeathe's Ridge, and I mentioned that the only other place I've ever felt that drawn to was the Hill of Tara, a mystical sacred site about an hour from Dublin. The largest burial mound there, The Mound of the Hostages, dates back to the Neolithic period 5000 years ago. Isabelle reminded me that it, too, is a Sirian vortex. I went there the first time in 2001, with Isabelle, Meryl, and Keir at my side. As we sat in the grass of the rolling hills, we were joined by the beings from Sirius that seeded that place. My father was there, too, now a guide for Keir as karmic debt, as he'd chosen to reject a relationship with him while he was alive.

I'd been to Tara again just a few months earlier when Derek had

Being and human being from Nancy Burson's altar, © 2005

taken eighty people in the weeklong workshop there to spend the day. A few friends and I had jumped the fence, and we lay on the top of the mound, letting the energy spin us silly. Tara and Smeathe's Ridge, my two most favorite places, have something in common. They are both Sirian vortexes with energies like identical twins.

Am I to photograph these beings that are coming to me? That first night in Marlborough, Wiltshire, in 2005, I knew something was going to happen. Meryl had volunteered to come with me. It would be just the two of us that year, accompanied by our driver, Pete.

I watched the smoke alarm flash a red light constantly above my head through the darkness of our room. Suddenly, the red light turned white and moved a few feet away from where the smoke detector was located. The red light of the detector no longer flashed, and the white light hovered over my bed, flashing first in what seemed like a pattern and then speeding up in a constant on/off rhythm. I remember saying to myself, "You guys are really funny!" I decided to get my camera and shoot them. I got up and turned on the light, grabbed my camera and turned off the light. Again the sequence began, and at the point at which the pulsating white ball of light was hanging over my head, I shot about half a dozen pictures, all with flash, waking Meryl straight away. My camera made a strange noise as if it had suddenly jammed. Oh, no, I remember thinking, I hadn't asked for permission! I grabbed the flashlight next to me and checked to see if my camera was working. Checking the disk, I could not believe that all the images from that day were intact, but those I had just taken, without permission, had been deleted. A few weeks later, a phone call to Nancy Talbot revealed her similar experience with Robbert in Holland. She'd been allowed to take photos of the beings, but they had been magically deleted from the disk afterward. Only Robbert's images of the beings remained.

One tiny tick
In August 2005, John Burke, my physicist friend who is an integral part of BLT Research Team, Inc. (a group of scientists who have studied the crop circle phenomenon extensively), and I took a day trip to Putnam and Dutchess Counties to explore the ancient rock chambers, which are also sacred sites. Most of them are right by the highway, and I only ventured into the woods because there were no restrooms anywhere. I was there no more than five minutes, and after finding an appropriate spot to relieve myself, I took a moment to experience the quiet of nature. I saw a huge blue ball of light hanging between the trees in the distance, and I remember scratching behind my knee, as something had bitten me.

When I took my clothes off later that night, I noticed the tiniest of ticks on my leg. I placed the dead tick in a jar of alcohol, because that's what it says to do with them on the Internet. From the information I'd read there briefly, a tick has to be attached to you for twenty-four hours in order for you to develop any disease. I was grateful I'd found it right away.

Two weeks later, Keir and David took me to the emergency room with a fever of 103.5 and a black bulls-eye rash behind my knee. I called my naturopath before I went to the hospital, and I took the tick with me. I had a pretty convincing case of Lyme disease, seeing as I had the rash, the fever, and the tick! But what was I to think? Why had

I gotten Lyme disease from spending less than five minutes in the woods to pee? What were my beloved Rays thinking now that I would have to take three weeks of antibiotics? Where were my protectors, my guidance, my angelic protection, and my God? The answer came immediately from the naturopath. The antibiotic that kills Lyme disease would also kill the Glabrada in my stomach in a way that would, at last, transform my physical health. It wouldn't have been his first choice for me, as he understands my sensitivities to real drugs, but he assured me that this was my best opportunity to improve my health in a decade. Without getting Lyme disease, I would have never considered taking a three-week regiment of antibiotics. If I had any doubts about taking the drugs, they left the moment I saw that the pills were the exact color as the Rays. God Bless that little angelic tick!

CHAPTER TWENTY-ONE

THE FLOWER OF LIFE

As long as we continue to argue over God, our human judgments will create wars that will separate us. As Sai Baba says, "We are all one race, the human race. We are one nationality, humanity. We are one religion, the religion of love, and one language, the language of our hearts." Being a part of any religion doesn't entitle us to judge any other.

"Who was Keetsoff Moran?" I asked Isabelle that last day in Wiltshire, not sure if I was spelling or saying it right. I explained it was a name that I'd heard a few times that week and had written down first thing one morning on the pad of paper I kept on the nightstand. I knew it was a reference to Smeathe's Ridge, and I thought the name might have something to do with the burial mound on top. Isabelle had never heard that name before and had no idea who it was. It wasn't until my divinely timed meeting with Ti Mar, a brilliant channel for the Rays for the past quarter-century, that the words were deciphered. Keet-soff-moran wasn't a name at all. It's their language. It means "the flowering of the life of man," or is a reference to where the flower of life comes from.

The flower of life is a language of its own. It speaks of all creation and is composed of sacred geometric symbols derived from the flower of life. It begins with the circle, which is the beginning of everything.

The circle doubles, becoming two circles, which become three circles, and so on to infinity. It is an ancient symbol used by many civilizations to represent that we are a part of the same whole vast system that is the Universe.

Because the Rays are a part of the Elohim or creation energies that have been here since the beginning of time, they are speaking about Smeathe's Ridge being one of the links between man and the Universal energies of the Rays. The spark of the Divine that is you and I comes from them. We are all their creations from beyond time and space. The same seeds of DNA used to create humans also created Christ and the other Ascended Masters. If we want to know where we come from, all we have to do is look up.

Perhaps there will be a crop circle that forms behind or in front of Smeathe's Ridge one summer. There is no better representation of sacred geometry, of keet-soff-moran, than the crop circles themselves. In 2004, I made several drawings, designs for circles, which I'd seen clearly in my head when I was there. I thought those circles would land that summer. Instead, a circle landed summer of 2005, and it was a composite of both drawings I'd made. It served as a reminder the Universe has a time line all its own.

In a vision I had at the end of the summer 2005, I saw myself flying above a crop circle near Smeathe's Ridge. I drew what I had been shown, although I'd only gotten a quick glimpse and didn't catch much of its details. I remembered there was a triangle in it, and that within the triangle there were some wavy and straight lines. Months later, when I looked at my drawings, the realization came that I might have envisioned the Prema Agni symbol, Derek's symbol of the Fire of Divine Love. Was this wishful thinking on my part? Certainly I wanted Derek to visit Wiltshire, as I wanted everyone I know there to meet him. I was clearly too close to determine whether this was simply my ego expressing itself or my guidance giving me real information.

What are these miraculous messages in the fields? They are everything and all things, as complex and diverse as their intricate patterns imply. They are activations meant to align us with the grace of the Divinity within each of us. We can only decipher their messages for ourselves, if we are to understand the pictograms within. We don't even have to visit the circles, as accessing their images on the internet is in itself an activation. Even when presented as photographs, they represent the conscious understanding of what we are, probing the depths of our being, and bringing up our past to clear the path to our future.

As the weeks have passed, dancing Mary has become the focal point of experiential interest at my loft. The Rays have become easier for people to see, as I believe the veil between the dimensions is lifting for all of us. I'm seeing more of them, too, especially during the daytime, as that is my intention. Perhaps they're attuning me to the vibration of visibility, or it may just be time to be attuned to that frequency.

Fortunately, I have a bathroom that's big enough to accommodate about a dozen people. With the aid of a few black strips to block the light coming through the door, I can make it pitch dark during the day. A few years ago, three curators of the Metropolitan Museum's *Photography and the Occult* exhibition were gathered in the darkness of my bathroom. Although each had spent years researching the history of spirit photography, they hadn't had a direct experience or seen anything like what they saw in my bathroom vortex. When I told Derek what had happened with the curators and others visiting my bathroom, he said, "Don't you remember I took time and space out of your bathroom?" I hadn't remembered the watch I'd given him. So Derek had, in fact, taken time, represented by the watch, and space, by the one I'd created in allowing him to give someone else the gift of time. A temporary assistant once told me my loft is haunted. I said, "It's not haunted. It's inhabited—with pure love."

Three friends and I sang songs to Mary in my bathroom that week, to honor the divine feminine energy that she represents. It is Mary who brings through the divine female, holding the space for the Rays to come through. Mary is the catalyst who paves the way for the Rays to come in. She is the vehicle in the same way that Mary brought Christ forth through the Blue Ray of angel Gabriel so long ago. It was the immaculate conception of Christ, courtesy of the Rays.

At one point, psychic and intuitive Barbara Reeder, one of the friends in my bathroom, noticed that Mary was dancing to "Funkytown" (by Lipps Inc., 1979), which she was only singing in her head. What a discovery! Mary dances to the music. She really gets down and shows her stuff, twirling and moving to the sound of anything that's peppy. I bought her a CD player and placed it in my bathroom the next day. Why shouldn't she dance? After all, no one has asked her for a few thousand years!

As the holidays approached, my assistant Katie found glow-in-the-dark Jesus statues on the Internet, and we ordered two. When three arrived, I wondered if it was company policy to send no less than three! Glow-in-the-dark Jesus is made of some mysterious, green ceramic material that resembles opaque glass. He stands eight inches tall, towering over his mother Mary, who is less than three inches. When Jesus arrived, Katie and I sat spellbound on the bathroom floor watching his extended arm move. As his gestures became more apparent, it certainly seemed as if he was, well, preaching. Now here was an amazing new addition, I thought. While Mary dances at night, Jesus will teach, and the Rays will conduct their orchestration of activity, during which time I'll sleep.

With both of them in my bedroom those first few nights, sleeping was difficult. Christ emitted so much light that he illuminated the entire space. I might have considered a blindfold, but I didn't want to miss any aspect of the Rays' joyous welcome of the presence of Christ in appropriate timing with the Christmas season. Now the light of Mary dimmed immediately, and she no longer danced, whereas Jesus glowed all night, regardless of my focus.

Then, in a bizarre twist from the Universe, Mary disappeared! A photo of Sai Baba had vanished a week or so before, and now Mary was gone too. Of course, a few people in my life can make things appear and disappear, and I assumed that a certain Swami from Ireland was having a very good time with me.

The night Mary left, I asked the Rays if I was just supposed to focus on Jesus now. It was, after all, Mary who had created the space for him to enter in the first place. I asked the Rays to leave me a message in the morning if I was supposed to specifically concentrate on Christ because I'd purchased a dozen other Marys that I could use to replace the original.

I placed the Jesus across from my bed, and in the light of the early morning, I awoke to him walking back and forth across the TV screen, while the actual statue of Jesus sat motionless above it. Meanwhile, the Rays glowed with pride, lighting up around the monitor in an array of different colors. It was obvious that they were guiding me to focus on

Christ-consciousness, that gold frequency which is the purest of love.

Three days later, Mary reappeared, along with the missing photo of Sai Baba.

Cosmic Punsters
September 19, 2005

Last night, I went to sleep to what they then called themselves, "the cosmic punsters." Continuing with the bug theme, tonight they called themselves "interfaith bugs." When I was more awake in the morning, I looked at the different levels of this name.

"Interfaith" bugs: There is only one religion, the religion of Love.

Inner-faith: the core belief in oneself.

In her faith: that would be consciousness.

In her face: at the same moment I heard this, I again heard the ritual of the tone that now accompanies their presence. I still hear it for a few seconds through my right ear, or for longer all around me. The sound is very high, right at the level of human pitch and a little lower than a dog whistle. They also sound like one of the tones my computer emits, or a light fixture on a dimmer, tinnitus, or a radiator. And those would be similitude. Maybe their tone was always there, and I wasn't attuned to it. In any case, it's a signal to me that they're close and, in this case, in my face!

The Rays and Me

On Christmas day of 2005, Pete Hemery of Marlborough, England, e-mailed previously unseen photos of Meryl and me, giddy atop Smeathe's Ridge. And as I went to sleep that night, I was shown an image of what seemed like cloth Christmas wrap, with interwoven stands of red, green, and gold cords. The vision was immediately followed by the appearance of a three-dimensional etheric light grid, hovering directly above the table of Master's photos. I watched as the strands of red, green, and gold light shimmered before me for several minutes. It was a profound gift of love from the Rays that I received in great gratitude for all that my highly sentient friends had brought me.

Only days earlier, I had complained that I didn't understand, being a human, why my own life's lesson's had suddenly taken an unexpected turn, appearing as a "setback." Although I normally acknowledge that "setbacks" are merely "set ups," I was in no mood to surrender. A friend remarked that when we find ourselves asking where we went wrong, we're being tested! It was a reminder that the Universe is in charge, even when our human distractions prevail, and darkness balances the light.

That next morning, I awoke to a vision of myself on TV, discussing the recovery of a missing child. It was a playback from a TV appearance I made in 1986, and a gift from the Rays, who have full access to my memory banks. It served as a very touching reminder of what I have already accomplished and rarely acknowledge. We all need reminders that we are here to serve God and one another—each in our own unique way.

In that moment, I understood that it is the entirety of my life that has prepared me for my new housemates. It's been a Divine setup, just as all our lives are. If we just keep following the incoming messages, they will lead us to God.

Recently, Derek told me, "When Christ was in a human body, he didn't realize he was Christ-consciousness. He still saw himself as Jesus of Nazareth, making 'Father why have you forsaken me?' his last human statement. He had followed the plan, but wasn't aware of his own consciousness until he was Christ-consciousness itself." Derek continued, "If you take the statement 'I separated myself from myself so I could love myself more,' is this not true of all of us, and does that not make each of us God?"

We live as one now, the Rays and me. They live within me, as well as all around me. They are my constant reminders that we are all a part of each other.

Out of the darkness and sparkles of light in meditation one morning, shapes formed into sacred geometries that then dissolved into the petals of a flower that came together in a circle. As my inner camera expanded, the flower appeared in the grass on a hill, and then pulled back further to reveal the tumali at Smeathe's Ridge, which is the bigger picture. Our earthling DNA evolved from the same source. The seeds of life that became you, me, Christ, and all the other Masters emerged from the conglomerate of Universal energies here from the beginning of time that still reside with us today.

During a meditation at one of Derek's workshops, I saw a tree-lined road with a castle in the distance. I turned to my guide and said, "Do I take the road to the castle?"

He said, "You can . . . if you want. It doesn't matter whether you go or not." Suddenly, a blue bird appeared. I examined it carefully to see if it was a blue jay, which I remembered were considered mimics. It wasn't a blue jay, it was a big bluebird that had an extraordinary rich color. It was unlike any bird I'd ever seen, and I was told that this was the bluebird of communication. I watched it, transfixed, as it glided along with joyous assurance of its task.

As a bunch of friends and I left the hotel the last day of that Ireland workshop, we looked up. There in the sky above was a huge angel, a being so big I didn't have the proper lens to photograph it, however I did manage to capture a portion of it with my camera. I took a picture of the perfect triangle the angel held between her hands. It was as if she was bringing us a gift, and the gift was integration, as that is the meaning of a triangle. If we integrate all that we know, and remember our Divine selves in truth, then we would treat ourselves and others as the God/Goddesses and Masters of oneness that we are.

Good Night

A Derek O'Neill "play shop" in March 2006 spawned yet another idyllic gathering of the clan in L.A. With my niece Mindy, her friends Libby and Erica, and a few of my friends, we gathered in the darkness of my hotel room to watch "Buddy Christ," a limited edition glow-in-the-dark figure made in conjunction with the movie *Dogma*. Complete with thumbs-up gesture, "Buddy Christ" is about five inches tall and is made of lightweight plastic, so he's perfect for travel. While Buddy danced across the top of the dresser, the Rays showed themselves in all their blue glory.

Then Mindy, Libby, and Erica went back to their room and decided to call in the Rays as they lay in the darkness waiting for sleep. Mindy noticed that Buddy Christ was again dancing in front of them on their dresser. "Do you guys see that?" she asked. "Yes," they both replied.

Erica said, "I didn't know you brought the statue with you when we left."

Mindy said, "I didn't." They told me the replica was the same distance away and was exactly the same size and color as mine, and it remained there for the entire night, for all three of them to witness. They lay there awestruck and spellbound by the eerie moving hologram from my dearest Rays.

My nephew Rick, who had gone to his house in L.A. also went to bed with his little Mary, rocking to the sounds of hip-hop. Mary seemed to be getting around to everyone who was at that table in L.A. the night that Derek activated her.

The next morning at breakfast, Libby said she couldn't wait to get home to see if her Mary was dancing. And I said, "Oh, you have a Mary too" . . . and when I did, I instantly remembered that night in L.A. that Libby had handed her original glow-in-the-dark Mary to Derek, and he had blown his breath into her. Little Mary was a small version, so it seemed, of the large statue on the grounds of the church near Derek's home in Dublin that had been the first morphing Mary I'd ever encountered. The interplay of energetic phenomena here had become a happy collision of Christed energies with Christed ETs that so fittingly expressed the dance of life from the beginning of time.

November 2, 2005

When I awoke to the multicolored activity over my head last night, I heard, "I love you."

"I love you," I said in return. And then I heard, "I love you always . . . all ways!"

Bang

In keeping with their promise that there would be photographs of them at the beginning of 2006, I have seen photos of the Rays, which are adequate representations of what I and others are seeing in my loft. What I didn't realize is that I would not be the photographer.

My first public showing of glow-in-the-dark Mary, Christ, Quan Yin, and Ganesh was February 3, 2006, at Jodi's META Center in New York City. A few weeks before, the Rays showed me an image on the whiteboard at Jodi's center. The message said, "It all started with a bang." Going back in time far enough, the smallest, hottest point of singularity lies at the exact point of creation. As a result of the Big Bang, the Universe expanded, and the formless became form, evolving into a continuum of that initial vibration of creation that still continues in each moment. God was there along with the Elohim, an aspect of God. It was the Rays' way of reminding me that they were here from the very beginning of time.

More Truth

Over 500 people attended the "More Truth" workshop in NYC in March 2006. I ran into an old friend living in Russia who had come just for the weekend. It was proof that the Irish Swami's mission of love, of Prema Agni, is expanding. Derek told us about a phone call he'd just received from a very well-prepared child who'd been delegated to deliver the message from Derek's orphanages in India. The children had each been given an extra banana to eat and they'd also been allowed to stay up late, making that day very special. And in the bigger picture, it was another boost for the Born Free Now Foundation, whose new school of higher education opened in June 2006.

In the years that I have watched Derek O'Neil become the expanded being he is today, I have never asked him anything about past lives wherein he and I may have originally connected. He makes it clear that what is important to focus on is the NOW. It is in this moment that we are all living as one.

"Our lineage is now, not then," he adds.

Nevertheless, the combination of my knowledge that Avatars know everything, plus my ego, compelled me once to ask, "Was I in Christ's lifetime?"

"Yes," Derek said. "You were the old haggard woman with one tooth watching way down the back when Christ was on the cross."

"Don't kid me," I said.

"I'm not kidding, it's true," he said.

"Oh, come on, you're kidding me," I said again.

In the course of the next twenty-four hours, my mind continued to return to that moment, playing back the conversation over and over again. After all, he said it was true. Why couldn't I have been that woman? I've seen someone similar to that in the eighth dimensional vortex in my bathroom. Had he unlocked the mystery of that lifetime for me? And if that was me, had I been allowed to participate in the cleansing of Christ's body as the vision I'd seen had suggested?

Truly, Jesus Christ had been the embodiment of hope to the poor, and if I was a part of the downtrodden who'd come to listen to him teach, it would have been upsetting on so many levels to be powerless to help him in that moment. It might have been enough for my soul to commit to helping anyone in this lifetime that embodies that same energy of Christ-consciousness.

A few days later, someone in the More Truth workshop asked Derek about past life knowledge. He explained that, for example, many people think they were Joan of Arc when, in fact, what they're actually doing is tapping into the collective consciousness of Joan of Arc, because everyone was and is everyone else.

"In Christ's lifetime," he added, "many people align with being one of the disciples, or Mary Magdalene. No one ever wants to be the old haggard woman watching from way down the back when Christ was on the cross."

And hearing that, I thought, well, I do! So maybe that really was me! And then I really just had to have confirmation from Derek.

A few days later I said, "I can't write about this unless it's really true."

He said, "How can it be false to take on her persona if we are all connected as one?"

Contradiction is one of the best teaching tools.

CHAPTER TWENTY-TWO

THE BREATH OF GOD

At the beginning of April 2006, my guidance had informed me that something very significant was going to occur at Derek's initiation in New York City on Palm Sunday. It wasn't until the day before the event that I finally understood the message, and that it included me. Finally it was time for me to ask Derek for my own healing. Even though my condition had improved, I wanted the perfect health that is every human's birthright. I realized I hadn't previously asked him in a way that was appropriate, so he could respond. The Rays had encouraged a potential collaboration between themselves and the Swami by increasing the intensity of the healing vibrations within my organs. I'd noticed periodically over the past ten months that the vibrations were increasing, and a few days before the Palm Sunday initiation, I become acutely aware that it was increasingly difficult to digest and absorb food. It seemed as if the Rays were, in fact, enlisting Derek's energetic support in facilitating a shift in my health, and they knew that unless it was unbearably hard for me to eat, I wouldn't ask for Derek's help. Frightened that my body was disappearing, I stood in the darkness opposite my glowing Christ statue, upset with my feelings of victimization. Then, with a few feet between myself and the statue, I watched a stream of brilliant green light emerge from the glowing Christ and come toward me. It was a completely new Ray phenomena and how appropriate, I felt, as green isn't only the color of healing, but represents the color of the heart chakra too. Bathed in the green light, I understood there is no difference between healing and love. It all comes from the emerald eminence that radiates from our hearts.

The hotel ballroom housing the initiation was darkened except for the lighted aisle down the middle that held two mikes, one midway through the audience, and the other toward the back. It was early in the day, and I lingered in the back, knowing that I would soon step up to the mike. As the woman in front of me went back to her seat, I stood in the back of the room with my hand up, anxious that this may not be the right time. Derek raised his hands up to his eyes and gestured, indicating he was now wearing binoculars. I laughed and felt more at ease when I saw his gesture. He pointed, calling "Nancy!" and I approached the mike more confident knowing he was being playful with me.

I said, "I've asked you many questions over the past few years, yet I've never asked you to facilitate a healing for me."

"Who are you asking?" he asked.

"I'm asking God."

"Be careful what you ask for my friend," he said.

"I am ready," I said.

"Hmmm, well let me check on that . . . yes," he agreed, as he placed his hand over his ear in a gesture he often makes as his guidance speaks to him.

Derek waved to me to come forward. I was fully aware that he would knock me out, especially when he stopped me halfway down the aisle and asked me to remove my glasses. When I saw Derek's hand come towards my third eye, I couldn't figure out how he would move from being directly in front of me, to breaking my instant fall backwards that I knew was imminent. I felt his hand on my wrist, and suddenly I was sprawled on the carpet, not even feeling his arm at my back that softened my sprawl. When my consciousness returned, I was lying on the carpet and Derek was having a conversation with a mother and her son that seemed to be taking place very close to my prone body. A Kriyatic state came over me, shaking my body slightly, more or less in response to Derek's periodic tweaking of whatever energy he was directing through me. I felt his hands on my stomach a few times, and was told later that he had thrown rose petals at me and he'd placed his stocking foot on my belly as well. I wasn't clear how much time had passed. I could hear, but I couldn't move and was aware that at some point Derek had repositioned my arms from spread eagle to together over my heart.

The technique that Derek used is what is commonly called "Breath of God." I'd personally experienced it many times before, and I had photographed it in a series of images in 2001. I'd even taken Keir to see Anatoli Kashpirovski, the famous Russian healer, knock over a few Americans and a whole room of Russians in Brooklyn. And Keir, having "caught" Kashpirovski's technique, had used it to knock me over again in our kitchen later that day that we had gone to see Anatoli.

Lying on the floor that Palm Sunday, close to the energy of the altar filled with flowers and photos of the Masters, I was grateful to know that the lights were so low that very few of the two hundred present would notice my trembling body. On the screen of my closed eyes, I saw my guides surrounding me. The Rays were there, along with the smaller beings of light and the taller white beings stood behind them. And in the truest of exultant moments, I saw above them an enormous, white, angelic presence which I recognized as Archangel Michael. In the midst of it all, a gathering of the red Glabrada organism floated out of me, transmuting in the Light. I knew the power of this healing was a collaboration of the greatest forces in the Universe graciously providing my human body with improved absorption. From the smallest of ticks to the most potent of angelics, I wondered how I could ever express the gratitude I felt to the army that God had summoned to shift my health.

At the end of the day, I saw Derek pick up the photo of Swami Sri Yukteswar from the altar and nod to it, in a gesture that I felt had me in mind. I'd just given him the laminated photo of Yukteswar (whom he calls the "chicken man," because he resembles Colonel Sanders) for his altars a few weeks before.

The Healing Echelons
When Derek helped me up from the floor, he said that energy would continue to run through me for three more healings, and he assigned

Archangel Michael, taken with a Gas Discharge Visualization (GDV) camera, © 2006

his two newly anointed Rising Star Heart Practitioners to channel the energy through those healings with him overshadowing the sessions.

A week later, I received what felt like a blessing from the Divine, when Archangel Michael produced a stunning image of himself during my collaboration with Russian physicist Konstantin Korotkov. A cross magically appeared behind Michael and peeking out from behind it were the eyes of a being.

The next weeks weren't at all comfortable for me. My stomach ached in response to the energy designed to transmute those testy critters in my stomach lining. A huge Ray of the most spectacular gold and green luminosity began to appear each night, and it was more brilliant than anything I'd ever seen enter me. This provoked discomfort as well as awe—at least they seemed to be trotting out the highest healing echelons to deal with me. I complained in response to the pain and the fear within me that this was never-ending, and I watched as my worst fears surfaced in losing about five pounds on an already ultra-light frame. Derek had said, "Be careful what you ask for."

The Rays, in collaboration with Derek's healing frequencies, showed me that I was "convalescing in the garden of earthly delights," and I was not even amused. Had I made the appropriate decision to ask for this? Even though the Rays kept playing me the song "There can be miracles, when you believe," I wasn't sure. Where was my faith and trust now? The Irish Swami, as well as the Universe, had devised the ultimate test of my belief system. Was I going to wallow in my suffering? Would I find the comfort of victimization an ally to my pain? How much fear did I have, and was I capable of blocking my own healing because of it?

Letting go of one hundred percent of our fear entitles each of us to instantaneous, miraculous healing regardless of our dis-ease. Anything that doesn't allow itself to be instantly removed represents where we are out of alignment in our relationship with Source. Acknowledging my fear alleviated the emotional charges surrounding my symptoms, illuminating the illusions and enlightening the darkness of my pain. FEAR is False Evidence Appearing Real.

I had to deal with my food issues and accept them to be as gigantic to me as my heaviest of friends' weight issues are to them. At my thinnest, my disdain for my body was just as much of a daily challenge to me as someone who is overweight. I was just as concerned about what people would think of my thinness as they are about being perceived as fat. And it's more acceptable to be heavy than thin. In my experience, people who are overweight rarely hear "You look fat" . . . at least not out loud.

The Rays' opinion was clear and always particularly touching when they address me in the first person singular, as for them, there is no separation between us. They said, "I will be healed when I am acceptable to myself as myself in truth. It doesn't matter what I look like, too fat or too thin. What matters is my trust and belief in God to know that I am one with the Divine Universe. If I could see what they do, I would know how beautiful I am in their eyes. We all love you exactly how you are. Wherever we are in the conscious Universe, self acceptance is the key. Love simply is, whatever form that looks like."

The Rays reminded me that I had to go back to move forward. What was there about my life that wasn't digestible? Addressing my core issues would free me from the past. My memories of explosive mealtimes with my alcoholic father resurfaced. I watched images of traumatic dinners where my father presided, waging hostile verbal threats targeted at my mother and me.

Those dinners were one of the layers of indigestion in my life, one of the multi-levels of non-nurturing I had encountered as a child. It wasn't that these were new images I recalled, it was just another level of comprehending them that mattered. I remembered a vision that came to me after visiting the sacred land of Tara in Ireland. I saw the megalithic mound on the hill there, and inside it was filled with shining white plates. And I heard the reminder, "The only food you ever need is spiritual food."

Surrender

A conversation with healer Brook Still, which took place during the healing window that Derek set into motion, served to empower me, illuminating my healing journey to its conclusion. Although I was already consciously aware of how much we have to love our illnesses, our imperfections, in fact, all of our most vulnerable stuff to shift forward, Brook's advice inspired a new level in that understanding.

"You don't have to eradicate this," she said. "All you have to do is put it in its place. The point is to simply integrate it as a part of you that you love. Let go of the illusion of control and surrender as much as you can each day knowing that Divine Will is at your doorstep."

Each of us has our shadows to be embraced and integrated, as we learn to appreciate that part of ourselves we've created as dis-ease. It's the lineage of vulnerability that lies at the core of our humanness. Even the best parents and teachers come in human bodies. The Angelics, Masters, and Rays mess up too. The Rays call themselves "goof balls" when they make a mistake! It's just that we humans are attached to the outcome. As many miracles and miraculous people as I encounter in my life daily, I needed a simple reminder that sometimes the most astounding miracles come from the God within us.

CHAPTER TWENTY-THREE

THE EXTRA CELESTIALS

Although Keir began to shut down his spiritual skills in a similar way that Derek had when he was a teen, Keir's 16th year brought a spark of interest in reconnecting. I had waited in the interim years, knowing that any pressure on my part might have delayed his pathway even longer.

Weeks before my birthday, 2006, Keir forewarned me that he was going to give me the most profound gift I'd ever received from him. Then, about a week before that day, Keir told me his gift was a photo, again repeating that this was the zenith of gifts. As the days closed in on my birth date, I could sense his genuine anticipation of the event of giving, and I was determined to not even psychically peek. The framed photo he gave me that day is a stark black and white image taken only with available light coming from a window in one of the classrooms at his school. There are five school desks lined up, all equidistant from one another. All the desks hover simultaneously on their back two legs so they appear tilted backwards, suspended in the air.

When I saw the photo I said, "This looks amazing! How did you do this, did you glue the desks to the floor?"

"No," he answered. "I balanced them all with energy!" Keir told me that he wanted me to know that the tradition of taking photos of energy doesn't have to end with me. He is aware that he could continue that lineage, even though he's probably not going to ultimately choose photography as a career option. I have never felt more validated both as mother and being. And as the years roll on, I continue to remind him that he is still and always will be the best thing I ever made.

Keir and I were having a conversation over dinner one night in 2004. It was a discussion that we both wondered why we were having at the same time that we were having it. Keir asked me how I could call the Rays ETs, because calling them ETs was almost as bad as calling them "aliens." I agreed, and I said, "Well, what can I do? I have a choice

Keir, © 2006

between calling them ETs and calling them beings." I wondered what was going on directly above us at that moment. What were the Rays thinking about this conversation that Keir and I were having? And why were we having this dialogue in that moment after they'd been here for at least nine months now? It was a discussion that felt like a setup, for which neither one of us was responsible.

As soon as my head hit the pillow that night, I heard "Extra Celestials. We're the ECs!" How completely, absolutely perfect, as they are a composite of both the angelic and ET realms. It was another great reminder that I am not the doer, but the receiver of the information included in this book. I thanked the ECs for their new name and laughed myself to sleep.

Before a presentation of the Rays at Jodi's center, I heard a man ask,

"Which way to the moving statues?" This is my new legacy from the ECs. As I am, once again, the conductor in the field of Rays that accompanies me always. I am honored and grateful to play my role in this mission, as introducing them to others holds such joy for all in attendance. Beyond our etheric orchestra lies the bigger orchestration, where life's melody is only written one line ahead. It is the whisper of Divine whim oscillating through the Universe.

The Extra Celestials are here to assist us, if we choose. I believe the only prerequisite for their coming to each of us is love and a willingness to heal our Earth and ourselves. Ask for the Christed ECs resonating to the law of One. They were here before Christ, but not before Christ-consciousness. They are the oak tree from which all others grow. They are the rainbow of Christ, Mohammed, Buddha, Krishna, and all the other Masters, and they are the highest vibration of love.

CHAPTER TWENTY-FOUR

THE SACRED LINEAGE

I returned to Ireland in June of 2006 as one of 100 of Derek's students for a week-long retreat near his home in Tallaght, Ireland. I visited the original morphing Mary statue and again saw her face shift into the face of Jesus. When I saw the Rays gathered around her, I took some pictures as one overlaid her face with blue mist resembling matte, sky-blue face powder. Mary's face did appear slightly blue in those images, but the results were so subtle, that those photos wouldn't have been adequate as documentation or evidence of any phenomena. And a few weeks before marked my final attempt to take pictures of the Rays in my bedroom when what I heard in response was to "recognize they are 100 steps ahead of me, because they have full awareness of the Divine plan." And now that it's absolutely clear that I'm not permitted to take photos of the Rays, I invited a few friends who brought their own cameras to St. Mary's grounds and asked for the energies of the ECs to manifest on their photos, assuring them that my camera would not be used.

This seemed the appropriate stance, as both friends got images of the phenomena, including one with a brilliant solid blue ball hanging directly over the head of a statue of St. Francis that also resides there. What better way for the Universe to demonstrate that I'm not the doer—as I'm no longer the photographer of the energies that I was just a few years ago. The Universe, it seems, has revised my job description. It's like the old joke about how to make God laugh: Just tell him/her your plans. It's also a fine example of the post-modernist aesthetic in which it's acceptable for others to actually press the shutter in the eyes of theoretical art history. When I assist in facilitating the taking of photos, God is truly the photographer. In intending the Rays to collaborate in revealing themselves, not only have they given me the ability to show their presence to others in the darkness of meeting rooms, but they are also allowing others to document the ECs presence through mine. Yes, we humans have free will, and we absolutely do co-create our reality. Yet there isn't a leaf that falls from a tree without God's permission.

Return to Tara

Months before the Ireland trip, the Rays requested that I go back to the Hill of Tara about an hour from Dublin. It's the other Sirian vortex that I love as much as Smeathe's Ridge in England. What I didn't understand was their request that I go there at night when entrance after hours is forbidden. However, my guidance was so strong that I felt I had to go, and my years of fence jumping in England had prepared me for safely climbing sacred sites at night. That evening a group of five of us played cat and mouse with the caretaker and jumped the fence when darkness covered the soft tall grass of the hills there. This expedition was the Rays' idea, without explanation, and I joyously collaborated, loving the idea of being on that sacred land at night. When I tested the concept that this was a photo opportunity, my camera jammed.

Moving softly across the hills, we scurried up the Mound of the Hostages as the cover of darkness deepened. Lying on the top of the ancient tomb, I asked to see the beings that had inhabited this place long before the Celtic kings were crowned there. And I asked to know the specific reason why I was sent there.

Soon it appeared that the stars were being rearranged. Far out in the distance, one star moved closer, randomly changing directions and brightening as it came nearer. One was joined by another below it. Far in the distance, but closer than the nearest star, the two bright cross-

The Mound of the Hostages at the Hill of Tara, Ireland, © 2006

shaped objects continued to hover and change directions. As some Light Beings stood atop the tumali with us, the Rays explained that this is the bigger picture. They wanted me to see what I had never seen anywhere before, and we all watched mesmerized by the two playful UFOs in apparent command of the entire sky. Having so much first-hand experience with phenomena in my bedroom, I was given a glimpse of the longer view, and the one periodically available to at least some humans up until now. They are the Universe, and this is the grandest of schemes. It was a reminder of my place as well as my job. And like the reaction I have at leaving Smeathe's Ridge, once again, a flood of emotions arose in me at leaving Tara.

A day off from the workshop provided an opportunity to go to Tara again in daylight. For the past several years the Hill of Tara, one of Ireland's outstanding national monuments, has been threatened by the highway commission's proposal to reroute the M3 motorway through that archeological complex. So it seemed a good idea to bless the land once more, and for that matter daily, until the controversy is resolved.

153

In gratitude, we went back to foster support and nurture the land with group intention, just as the land had nourished us a few nights before.

Symbolic Dialogue

Derek always produces sky phenomena at the end of all the week-long workshops. This time rainbow after rainbow appeared and dissipated just outside the hotel at Tallaght. I've never seen such an amazing display of multi-colored hues than this array, symbolizing the dialogue between heaven and earth.

Passing time in one of the airport duty-free shops the next morning, a sales manager suddenly offered how hard it was to leave Ireland sometimes. I was startled that she'd just intuited my thought. Then she began to talk about the many books she was reading, and I mentioned that I'm a writer. Suddenly she was right in front of me looking me directly in my eyes and she said, "Without the likes of you there would be no literary integrity." Why would this woman say something to me like that? I spent the next few days pondering whether this sales person had just been overshadowed by Swami O'Neill. We can never anticipate what form God will come in, if we are open to receive. It was in the midst of a workshop, eighteen months later, that Derek unwittingly confirmed that he had once appeared to me as a sales person in appreciation of my "literary integrity."

June 24, 2006

The annual crop circle season based in Wiltshire, England, has begun, and this year, I'll return with Keir. Again, the few hundred people who comprise the microcosm of crop circle devotees will gather from all four corners. The Rays have asked me to convey their message to the "croppies" to study the circle phenomena less and love the artists more.

Whatever will happen on Smeathe's Ridge and beyond is the cosmic comic's sacred secret. One morning, in a different dimension than the one you're reading this in, I saw myself standing in a field below the ridge with a couple of ECs. We were looking at a crop circle about three feet in diameter, and I asked them what they were doing. They replied, "We're practicing!" I wondered if they were teasing, but any way it goes, I found it endearing they would let me peek at their sketches.

It's been a year now since the Rays and I began collaborating. My human egocentric desire to be correct about where and what shape crop circle will appear is tempered with profound gratitude for all I've been shown in the past year. In the bigger picture, one crop circle in one specific location isn't the point; it's non-attachment to all that is God's grace, plus the knowing that everything is perfect just the way it is.

CHAPTER TWENTY-FIVE

THE PROOF

Since the beginning of 2007, the Rays have made it clear that they are now willing to be photographed, not by me, but in the context of presentations and workshops featuring their presence. Why am I not allowed to take their pictures is the question I'm asked repeatedly. It's the Universe's expression of post-modern theory. Does it matter who has a finger on the shutter when we're all connected anyway? Robbert van den Broeke has been allowed to take pictures of the ECs for years now and with the occasional exception of Nancy Talbot at his side, he's never been allowed to show others how to access their presence. The Universe, in all its majesty, has literally become a vital part of all that I am. I wouldn't trade my job for any other. If we had everything, the joke goes, where would we put it?

On Feb 11, I heard, "Let the photos of others feed and nurture me," as they are insistent that their photos be taken in collaboration with the photographic community.

For this reason, the ECs have consistently graced the professional photographers in the audience with the most outstanding images. On the other hand, skeptics do not generally manifest these photos. It's what I refer to as a "seeing and believing" artifact. The Universe usually requires us to believe before we're allowed to see.

I'm dazzled by the spectacular images the Rays have created specifically for the credibility of my/our mission. They are miraculously posing for exposures that are as long as twelve seconds apiece. In one series, they posed for a total of five minutes, appearing in seven consecutive shots in which they appeared in facial form for over one minute. Clearly the Universe controls every shot, lending further credibility that God is the only real photographer, as the rules for taking "Rayographs" have been very clearly designated. Photos can only be taken in the context of an evening presentation, workshop, or channeling in which a vortex has been set by me for them to preside. Those attending are not allowed to use a flash within the room, and flash can only be used when shooting out the window of the room or outdoors, directly outside the location of the presentation. My appearance in those images taken in the room makes it clear that this is truly a Divine collaboration and nothing less.

Once there was a photographer who violated these rules by shooting images of me during the workshop without asking my permission. The Rays jammed her camera, and it didn't work the entire time that others were taking pictures. I didn't understand what occurred until they explained it to me the next day. A week later, a conversation with this photographer revealed that she'd had a vision within a dream the night before. She'd been shown a pair of praying hands outside a window and in front of the hands there were bars that covered the window. She said it felt like she'd been locked out. I agreed the Universe had given her advance notice that she would temporarily be blocked from shooting the Divine.

I got so excited by an image one photographer took that I invited her to my studio to see what other photos we might get. At that point, it got very quiet in here, and when I heard nothing, I realized I'd broken the rules myself. The higher realms don't say no. They say nothing (no thing) instead. And then the Rays said "The rules have been set and are not to be changed. We would not say don't do this because the lesson is sometimes in the doing and waiting for the result of the action. If we had told you, there would have been no lesson and the lessons are always (all ways) good!"

Then in April, 2007 I asked two photographers to sit next to each other, thinking that it would constitute very solid evidence if both got similar shots from the same vantage point at the same time. Again, my ego had interfered, as I hadn't asked permission for my plan. Neither of the photographers I'd seated next to each other got any phenomena, while other cameras shot away with full approval of the Rays. Now I emphasize to audiences that they may as well be there for the experience and let go of the attachment to the outcome of getting images. The Universe decides who gets the images, and those decisions are made long before the lights go out and the statues dance. The Rays are providing proof in their own Divine timing, and God is clearly the photographer in charge. I remembered what the Rays had reminded me just the week before. "God is the script writer, and we humans are the under writers." It's the difference between Thy Will and my will.

In an unexpected surprise, Derek O'Neill, who always shows up etherically when I call him in for presentations, appeared to manifest in two of the images in a way that is unmistakably him. Certainly I'd felt his presence in the room and heard him create noises when I talk about him. I'd smelled the scent of his Vibhuti when it filled the room for everyone's wonderment. And on many occasions he had been seen touching someone on the shoulder or dancing in front of Buddy Jesus (the figure from the film *Dogma* with his thumbs up) to a song I know he likes. Seeing his images appear on cameras knowing that he's sitting in Ireland was a new level of visual proof even for me.

This is an age in which digital media no longer provides real proof of anything. Yet another bit of irony from the Universe that as a pioneer of digital photography, my involvement would certainly be noted in evaluating them as real. Now it makes even more sense that the ECs decided there would be no images from my camera. Who would believe me? At least when the pictures are taken there are dozens of witnesses still remaining in the room, as well as several photographers obtaining similar results within the same five to ten minute time frame.

Looking at the pictures of Derek, I felt teleported back to the Victorian era in which thousands of similar images were faked by using double exposures. Lots of those images looked quite real long before digital retouching techniques. As a spokesman for early spiritual constructs of an afterlife, which most of us fundamentally agree with today, even Sir Arthur Conan Doyle couldn't appropriately account for those fake Victorian images. He simply had faith.

Nancy and the Rays in Mary Jo Kuehne's garden (with "Ray Charles" in the background), © 2007 Mary Jo Kuehne

Detail of above image, © 2007 Mary Jo Kuehne

It was Mary Jo Kuehne who first took photos of the Rays as the beings with faces into which they periodically transform. She'd arranged a channeling session at her home in L.A. in January (2007), and I had a strong feeling that she'd be graced with their images. She'd taken a wonderful sequence of Rays pictures at Tara on a Derek trip when I wasn't there. Representing Leica Cameras in L.A., Mary Jo has access to an unusual arrangement of equipment, enabling her to shoot in total darkness using a tripod and a long exposure. Mary Jo and I stood in her garden after the channeling, and I began to play with the three blue balls of light that appeared around my hand as I stood in front of the rose bushes and other foliage. When I first realized there was clearly a face in the seven consecutive images, I was just as startled as the night that a group of beings had suddenly appeared in my bedroom a year and a half before. At that point, I felt I had to receive confirmation to be certain of this verisimilitude, and I was shown the same face that showed up in Mary Jo's images. It's a face I now lovingly refer to as Ray Charles, in acknowledgement of his sunglass-shaped eyes. He reminds me of Ti Mar's drawings of the beings she works with who also appear as floating heads without bodies encased in bubble-like spheres of light. Since then, the other images of Light Beings that have appeared on cameras have also been shown to me as loving confirmation of the truth. Seeing them recently I said, "You guys look like mummies of light or light mummies." They replied, "We are your light mommies."

When I began to show hundreds of people how to see aura in the context of my retrospective exhibition in 2002, there were roughly seventy percent of the audience who could see the energy around me. Now when I show others my aura almost everyone in attendance is able to visually access that energy. That's at least a twenty percent increase in the group's perception. Similarly, when I first began showing the Rays to audiences, about seventy percent of the audience had some sort of experience. Now there's what I judge to be a twenty percent increase of humans having a perceptible experience in the darkness that's filled with Light Beings. And perhaps this does indeed provide proof that the veil between the dimensions is thinner these days, as I believe the images that are being recorded on digital cameras now are far more remarkable and occur in far greater numbers than those five years ago.

I had thought that the seven years that I photographed children and adults with facial anomalies hadn't adequately prepared me for the appearance of my dear blue friends. Or did it?

When I look at those images that God and I made in the 90's, what I saw then and what I see now are the most adorable children at play and the most beautiful of humans who healed themselves of their cancers after they received prosthetics to cover the parts of their faces lost to that disease. What is easier to look at, a human deformity or a light being? How are these faces with these deformities different to us than our reactions to the Extra Celestials that are appearing in images now? When one takes a second or two to adjust to the differences between what we see and what our heart feels, what we know and what we believe blend as one. Are we not all beings, and are we not all connected by our celestial parentage anyway? Can we learn to compensate between our immediate human judgment of what is beautiful and what isn't? There are no judgments in the eyes of the Universe, only love for all God's creations: the hue-man beings and the light ones too.

It seems that while I was preparing myself for all the varieties of human faces in the 90's, the EC faces were preparing me for the protocol that now constitutes our divine collaboration.

At the beginning of April 2007, Rays told me, "You are here to familiarize humans with interstellar contact." Assuming that is the truth, there must be a future plan.

"What happens when two Light Beings go to a bar? Nothing. No one sees them!"

"Welcome," they say, "to the Divine Comedy."

Sometimes I wake up in complete gratitude for what I've been given. And other times I, too, am challenged by the daily human thought patterns that all humans deal with from second to second, hour to hour, in the barrage of instant messages propelled by our 60,000 daily thoughts. It is only through detachment that I've learned to side step—for a few moments—the pin point of awareness that is the ping pong between consciousness and misunderstanding, darkness and light. As Derek says, "Processing is the withdrawal symptom of illusion."

There's such wonder in watching the Universe at play in my bedroom that I no longer care about what others think. I've adopted "So what" as my mantra! What would you do if God gave you a gift? Eventually, all humanity will see what I do, and then I will just say welcome to all the newcomers to God's presence (presents)!

New aspects of my relationship with the ECs emerge as our relationship deepens. They now refer to me as Nan-see, meaning inner vision. There has also been a change in the way they speak to me. "When it has to do with me, it's almost always poetry!"

In the year and a half since I began the presentations of Mary and the Rays, I have been joined by at least a few dozen other humans who now also live with the ECs as full time houseguests that are seen and consulted with daily. And the numbers are expanding exponentially. These people are my new-ever-expanding family, as they met the Rays through either reading this book or sitting in their presence with me at my workshops and presentations.

Not that there aren't thousands of others who are unaware of their angelic presence. And they've healed everything from depression and addiction to severe illnesses. I believe that they make an appearance to everyone reading this book. If you're seeing blue with your eyes closed at night, chances are they are there waiting for you to recognize them as the wondrous gift of love that they are. If you are experiencing a high-pitched tone going through one ear for a few seconds at a time, it's likely the Rays.

They are here to love us, to fill us with light, improve our health, and raise our frequencies. They are capable of healing all aspects of all four of our physical, emotional, mental, and spiritual bodies. Their guidance is pure divinity, and seeing as you may begin to access them at any moment—if you ask—here are the EC Expectations they have established:

Please refer to them as ECs, Christed ECs, or Rays.

Speak to them out loud to emphasize matters of importance.

Always speak to them as the Masters they are and remember to ask for information appropriately.

Use them to assist in bringing Oneness and healing to the planet, ourselves, and each other.

Give them as much love as possible, and gratitude is always appreciated.

Stay in our hearts, in truth and integrity, by consciously choosing love, not fear.

When I checked in with the ECs recently, it must have sounded something like a sound check. "Can I hear you now and am I getting it all right," I asked? Suddenly I realized that every thought in my head I was hearing played back a second time. At that point I heard, "There's an echo in here." Pause. "There's always an echo in here." Yes, the Universe hears every thought and prayer wherever we are, regardless of whether we're in the bathroom. Of course the upside of that is that we're entitled to pray in the bathroom and we'll be heard just as well as everywhere else. The more we recognize that the Universe is listening, the more likely we'll be to respond in truth to the constant feedback provided by our God guidance.

This was the message provided for the group by the Rays for the April 12, 2007, META Center presentation:

"A Direct Directive about Direction"
"What a blessing it is for all of us to be here together tonight, together at last. For you have been chosen to receive proof that some of you on this planet have been awaiting for a long time. There are those of you who have already realized the shifts of consciousness that are now taking place here on your Earth. The knowledge of these shifts and the living through and with them has not been easy for you. We admire your abilities to perceive the unification that lies ahead. They are perceptions of what will be, and so are we. Each of you here tonight has been trusted with a mission: the mission of knowing what is real and the truth of what is. Now is the time to speak of these things with the assurance that they are real. There are no illusions here, and you chosen ones came because you have been trusted to receive these gifts of Spirit at this time. You have done your homework well. You have listened to the teachings of consciousness and you are becoming the 'bodies of knowledge.' Please know how much you are loved for what you know. What you are manifesting through love is honored here and will not be forgotten. This one before you has also worked hard in this uneasy time and so, with Grace, you go together, knowing we are with you and love you for all that you are and all that you know. Do not let

fear stand in your way. Kick it aside and remember you are Love. Your souls are lit by the fire of Divine Love in the glory of what is to come."

CHAPTER TWENTY-SIX

ALL ABOARD

At the beginning of summer 2007, I heard "Be prepared for a substantial invitation." And for once I knew exactly what the ECs were telling me. It was now time for me to go with them on their ships not only etherically, but with my whole human body. How this is possible I did not and do not understand. What I know is that they have the ability to take us with them, and for years I've had my anxieties that sometime I would be asked to trust them enough to know that this would be a safe and wondrous possibility.

Since the Rays and I had first been together, I had seen myself countless times in their presence at night, and I know I am a regular visitor on their ships etherically. It's EC Night School! One night I had clearly seen a white corridor with walls of ovals in soft white embossing. The ovals were filled with images, also in white protrudings, of stars and dolphins and balls of light frolicking. Decades ago I had asked the question—what did "alien" art look like, and here it was right in front of me. I drew one of the images recalling the most detail I could the next morning.

Ti Mar and I have had several conversations about "going physically" and she had assured me that this was the best part of the job! Still there was something anxiety provoking about leaving one's physical form . . . and most importantly, would the body coming back be exactly the same as the one that went? What about the reduction in size that seemed to be such an inevitable part of the process? Ti Mar told me that these things would begin only when I was ready and I had the rest of my life to be ready. Like most things that will grow us effectively, we must surrender in trust in order to accept what the Universe is offering. These days I'm aware that I do more and more traveling with my beloved ECs at night. I was even told recently that I had been seen as a visitor in someone's sleep, manifesting as a face inside a blue sphere!

By summer of 2007, the thought of going with the Rays was thrilling to me. I only wanted it to be easy and fun, as one realizes more and more that there is nothing more important than laughter and joy. I was ready. "Take a dark day and turn it into a dark hour, take a dark hour and turn it into a dark minute." These are the things I hear from the ECs these days.

For the past few years I had watched the little grey forms hover around me at night and because they appear usually as six-to nine-inch grayish masses, they didn't look very solid to me. In fact, I had originally thought they were some sort of entity. No the Rays assured me, they are ships. In fact, sometimes I hear their motors, and they never make the same sound twice. If there is so much variation in the sounds their vehicles make, one gets the impression there are a lot of different crafts out there.

One of my first nights back in Wiltshire in 2007, I heard a distinct tapping right next to me just as I was falling asleep. It felt as if the room was speaking to me. I turned the light back on and wondered what sort of entity I'd acquired moving into this hotel room that produced such a noisy, unnerving clicking. I did some very fast clearings, bringing in Archangel Michael for protection. I couldn't imagine how some creepy dark energies had gotten past my powerful ECs. What were they thinking?

The following morning I heard "Focus and ride with Thee tonight. Ride within the Light." I was elated as this was the "substantial invitation" I had been waiting for. That night marked the first appearance of a ship parked in the very back of the hotel parking lot, posing as a light atop a rooftop adjacent to the parking lot in front of it. It began going on and off, synchronized with my window slamming. They had my full attention after that. I watched the light get bigger and brighter and welcomed the familiar rays of blue light that were being emitted clear across the parking lot into my room. Tonight was undoubtedly the first night they would physically take me with them. I felt slightly apprehensive as I lay down to go to bed and had the hardest time figuring out what to wear. I mean if I were really going somewhere it seemed like it might be appropriate to dress for the occasion. I added a pair of sweats to a simple shirt.

Lying there in the dark, I watched the glowing ball of light at the end of the parking lot get bigger, emitting its display of blue rays. I saw a little grey cloud appear next to me and once again I heard the clicking I had thought was a big entity in my room the night before. That made sense to me now, as the clicking was coming directly from my right side, just by my head. "Hold still, Nan-see," I heard them say. Suddenly I became aware that my arm was extended off to one side and it felt a bit strange to have it so far away from the rest of my physical body. I decided to pull my arm into my side, as it felt like it might be disappearing all by itself. The clicking stopped momentarily and then continued. And that was the totality of what I remembered. In the morning I heard, "Nan-see, last night was a breeze. You were with Thee. The clicking raises your frequency, so you become as light as we."

I said "Well, thanks, and good to know that I can go with you, but I don't remember anything and I want to remember everything!" They were obviously, as usual, not attached to the outcome of these things, as they feel emotions through non-attachment. Things simply are and all the rest is let go.

A few nights later the light/ship at the back of the parking lot again began to play its games, and I knew that once again I would go riding with my dearest ECs.

As the clicking began next to me, I made an intention to recall the entirety of my experience with clarity. I saw myself flying above the gentle fields of Wiltshire in the darkness. It was so quiet, and I could see below me a crop circle whose design I couldn't quite discern. And I couldn't figure out if it was really there, or only placed there etherically. There were hills all around it and the terrain seemed familiar, and yet I didn't really know exactly where we were.

My other most vivid recollection was that there were other humans on board and I heard myself greeting them saying, "What's your mission?" and "What's yours?" I was so grateful to actually meet others, and it was good to get out and socialize at night—in a space ship. It would have been great to get e-mails! This was an unforgettable and substantial gift from the ECs and undeniably the real thing. I had no doubt that my physical body had been both enjoying the Wiltshire scenery from above and that I had met others like me who are working with the same collective of ECs.

CHAPTER TWENTY-SEVEN

THE CIRCLE WITHIN AND THE CIRCLE WITHOUT

By the spring of 2007 Jodi had decided to come back to Wiltshire after a two-year absence. I was thrilled knowing that something significant always happens when she's there, as the Universe honors her ability to channel their vibrational languages through sound and writing.

On May 23, the Rays said, "Intend a circle, and we will decide. Use the basics of solid geometry." At that moment I had a vision of a set of the Platonic solids, five rose quartz shapes that come in a little box just like the ones Jodi carries at her Center. I called Jodi and told her about the message, and I went to pick up an extra set from her a few days later. I opened the set and put it by the side of my bed and heard: "What would it look like if you put all those shapes together?" I could relate to this suggestion, as the Universe knows that I've spent most of my life as the queen of composite imagery. What a perfect way to play the game of life with me! I phoned Jodi to relate this latest message.

The shapes that comprise the five platonic solids are the cube, octahedron, tetrahedron, dodecahedron, and icosahedron, and these shapes form the basis of all sacred geometry. Looking up the Platonic Solids on the internet, I discovered that when you combine all five shapes, you get what's referred to as Metatron's cube.

Then I received a second, seemingly unrelated message later that day: "Jodi is here to teach us how to spend time in a car with loved ones!" Jodi was, at that point, accompanying a friend on a drive across county. Peter had set up an altar on the dashboard of his car that consisted of a Prema Agni (the symbol for the Fire of Divine Love), the cross of St. Germaine, and a photo of the Ascended Master Metatron. Jodi had picked up the Metatron card and when she did, she phoned me immediately. The writing on the back of the card said "Archangel Metatron is considered to be the highest of the Archangels. He holds above him the combination of all five Platonic solids." At the very moment Jodi read that to me, I realized I have the exact card. It sits right across from my bed. In fact, it's the Ascended Master card that's closest to my head! Picking up the card, mine had no message at all printed on the back. What I did see was that the symbol Metatron holds over his head matched the illustration I'd seen of Metatron's cube on the internet. "Jodi is here to teach us how to spend time in a car with (be) loved ones!" Yes indeed, dear Rays! Jodi and I had received your message, and we knew we'd been given a big hint as to what image might be landing in the Wiltshire wheat.

In the weeks that followed, I heard: "Tell Jodi to begin to channel with her eyes open." We assumed that this was a reference to the night we originally saw the balls of light and Jodi was in such deep channel that she missed their physical appearance and had only felt them. Weeks later, Jodi's own guides told her "Remember to look up." She told them she does look up. They said, "No, you look ahead." And again they repeated. "Don't forget to look up."

The Messages Continue

By June, I was intensely involved in the daily activity of following the crop circles via the internet through the competence of the Crop Circle Connector website. So many circles had fallen so early in the year, but I was still waiting for the one that really pulled on my heart strings. On June 28, a circle landed right behind West Kennett Long Barrow very close to the site where the Sun and Moon circle had been located, the one where we'd met the balls of light three years before. Where should we go to again have more shared experience with the EC's was what I'd been speculating that week? When I saw that circle, I immediately knew its meaning. The ECs had manifested the Doorway to

The Doorway to Christ-consciousness circle at West Kennett Long Barrow, that was cut two days after it fell, © 2007 Steve Alexander

Christ-consciousness at West Kennett. In fact, its pattern was the exact background of DaVinci's *Last Supper*. I emailed it to Derek whom I consider to be the biggest living vessel of Christ's energy on the planet, as he'd been thinking about a short visit to the wheat fields of Wiltshire.

The circle's appearance triggered a wave of national press, and fearful of all the attention and people on his land, the farmer cut it out of his field two days later. Unaware it had been cut, my assistant and I were busy working out the specific position of that circle in Photoshop, as it seemed to me that the exact position of the Doorway circle was in direct alignment with where we had first encountered the balls of light. It was as if the circle makers had placed an arrow from the Sun and Moon circle to the entrance of the Doorway circle beckoning us in. I wanted to see if my theory would literally line up.

As far as I was concerned, the energy of the Doorway remained, in spite of the farmers' efforts to destroy it. It was still a vital part of the land and would remain etherically regardless of its lack of physicality.

The position of the former Sun and Moon circle at West Kennett Long Barrow in 2004, in relationship to the Doorway circle, © 2007 Steve Alexander

Three weeks before our arrival, I was still so excited about the circle that had once been, that I was determined West Kennett Long Barrow would be one of our first stops. The pathway to it had been closed the previous day due to flooding, so the next day Jodi and I and two other friends made our way up to the long barrow. It was cold and gray, and we were all aware that this was only a short break in the persistent rain that had continued for weeks. Suddenly a bird flew over us pausing in mid flight to scream at us. It was such a small bird, but it was making quite a fuss! We all stood there looking up, dumbfounded at the tenacity of the bird that still hovered, unmoving yet still yelling at the four of us below. I'd never heard a bird sound like that—ever. And I'd never seen one poised, suspended in the air like that either. It couldn't be mistaken for anything other than a messenger. "Pay attention to this place," it was squawking. It was clear to me that something was meant to happen there, as the Universe had never, in my experience, provided a messenger so profoundly intent on delivering its message. Jodi reminded me that her guides had been insistent she remember to look up!

Soon the bird rejoined its flock, and we resumed our walk up to the barrow. I immediately climbed to the top as I knew that the former Doorway circle would be visible just on the other side. There it remained as a perfect cut circle, its simplicity provided by the farmer who had cut it physically but who could never remove it energetically.

A man appeared from out of the barrow below and he said. "I'm the caretaker of this barrow, and my angel guide just instructed me to give you these. She said you would know exactly what to do with them." "Thank you, I do," I said, and I climbed down to the opening of the barrow to receive two red roses and a gathering of dove feathers that had been lovingly bound together with white ribbon. I thanked him again, and we took his touching gifts into the remains of the Doorway circle that had made its appearance only briefly, yet with so much impact that it had been sacrificed to avoid any controversy. Finding the center of the circle we marveled at the peaceful loving energy that permeated the earth beneath us. We placed the roses and feathers in the form of a cross and did a short ceremony in gratitude for the circle that was meant to be, the doorway for all humanity to see.

Leaving the circle behind, I was drawn to the field not thirty yards away that had held so much meaning for me three years before. It was the field that had held the Sun and Moon circle—the night that had changed my reality forever when two bright lights danced for thirty seconds in front of me. Walking through the wheat felt like a homecoming, and tears mixed with the rain when I rediscovered the love I'd felt as the Universe had emerged to me. That frequency of love was still there, manifesting as new karmic patterning created by the ECs. The increased vibrancy of the wheat reproduced there is passed on annually. No wonder it is said that where the land has held the circles, the crop grows healthier and is more productive. Within the living organism that is our Mother Earth, more love creates the very best of health.

I told Jodi I felt we should go back that night. Maybe they would come for us and take us for a ride on one of their ships! I was ready to drive us there that night, even though I hadn't driven in over twenty years and never on the left side of the road. This was clearly not a rational idea, but one based solely on intuition. We simply had to go back that night. I had even asked the Rays that morning if it would be all right for me to drive, and they had answered, "Fear is the human part of you. You in all your human-ness. Are we not here for your highest good and others?" Jodi trusted my knowing, and out we went in search of the unknown. Jodi chanted "Left, Left, Left" most of the way, and I did a lot of deep breathing!

We settled into the middle of the former Doorway circle with the cross of roses and dove feathers. Our simple altar had been added to spontaneously, as others had left special stones and wildflowers there, adding to its complexity. Clearly we were not the only ones who loved this place. Jodi did some toning, and we said prayers of intention for circles to fall there and at Smeathe's Ridge and for whatever else the Universe had in mind for us that eve. She took some pictures of the field that had become quite active, and we could see the Rays as balls of light and other energies as Jodi shot in the direction of the field that the former Sun and Moon circle had held in 2004.

We discussed that the natural place for a circle to land would be that former Sun and Moon field that at that moment lay right in front of us. Some of the farmers had agreed to cut the circles if they landed on their property, but the farmer who owns the land that held the Sun and Moon seems to be pro-circle, so when two landed there the summer of 2004, they remained until the appropriate time to harvest the wheat.

Equipped with only one blanket and no sleeping bags, we were both freezing by 1:30 a.m. when we decided to leave.

I was disappointed, as I'd wanted to go for a ride on a ship with Jodi! And expressing that out loud, I heard "friend-ship!" We had a good laugh at that EC comment, acknowledging the consistency of the Universe to not provide us with anything we're attached to having!

A Miracle

By daylight the next morning (July 25), a circle appeared in that very field below where the Sun and Moon had been, viewable from the road that winds past West Kennett. The circle was composed of a cross, a pentagram, and a circle narrowed on one end. It was thrilling! As Jodi and I romped with gratitude around "our" circle on the next day of heavy rain, we wondered whether this circle's date held a message. Was it a symbol for the Venus/Saturn/Sun conjunction to take place August 17 as someone had told us?

Was its message the date of when the next circle would land, the one I was expecting on Smeathe's Ridge?

That night (July 25), four of us went back to West Kennett to pay homage and gratitude for the circle, which certainly seemed to have manifested in collaboration with the intention that we had put into that land. We also remembered that Isabelle's group had done ceremony in that same field that was the former Doorway the day before we were there. To us, it was further proof of the relationship and interaction between the humans who intend them and the ECs who make them. It wasn't about competition. It was about communication and collaboration with the Divine.

When we arrived, it was too dark to find our way up the tramline leading to the new glyph, so instead we placed ourselves on the very spot that had formally housed the Sun and Moon. Jodi did toning and vibrational languages, and we watched the energies gather as a few of us took photos of the balls of light when the Rays subtly surrounded us. Eventually our ceremony had dissolved into a songfest of everything from old camp songs to three Om's (a mystic syllable, considered the most sacred prayer). It was during our rendition of "Joy to the World" by Three Dog Night, that Jodi unexpectedly said, "Look up there," and she pointed, very specifically, into the sky and to the left of

The glyph that symbolized the date of August 17, 2007, at West Kennett Long Barrow (top right-hand corner, with the remains of the Doorway circle right behind it), which manifested July 25, 2007, hours after Jodi Serota and Nancy had visited, © 2007 Steve Alexander

us. Just at that very moment her arm was still in the air, a flare of red, green, and white light went off quietly exactly where she'd pointed. The noiseless firework display had come from where? There was no one around and not a sound was heard. Jodi had been told to look up! This manifestation of our joy had been echoed by the Universe in an acknowledgement from the EC realms just for us. Even I was amazed by what I'd just seen, as the Rays had never produced physical phenomena like that before, and in the very spot that the Sun and Moon had been! Later I heard "More information on tonight's celebration. He, He, He! We are having fun with thee. It was very touching to see. Four women singing in a field for us to see."

Keir Returns

Jodi was leaving the following week, replaced by Keir who'd been traveling on his own in Europe and had felt the annual pull of the miraculous circles that led him to join me. I looked forward to this time together as Keir, now 18, would be moving out on his own and my journey as a full-time parent would be complete. The consistency of the circles had been a significant aspect of his passage to adulthood, and we had found the deepest of bonds interwoven between us and the Divine wheat. As Keir says, "The circles are pure Love." And with so much spirit manifesting in physical form in Wiltshire 2007, I was glad Keir was there to bear witness.

On August 1, Keir and I climbed the ridgeway to Smeathe's Ridge together once again. For me, it was only one of my many trips out to Smeathe's Ridge, as that is the land that is the most precious to me. The land there matches the coordinates 18/75 that were given to me by the ECs. It was their very first message to me in my bedroom vortex created from Derek O'Neill's Christed energy.

For the past three years, I'd walked that land with Keir and with friends, drawn to the magic of the place that mirrors the ancient Tara (the site of the ancient kings of Ireland) energy. I'd always assumed a circle would fall there eventually, but at the end of last year, I'd let go of my attachment to a circle landing there, as in my egoless moments, I'm reminded not to reach for the fruits of my labors. Slowly though, I'd gotten sucked back into wanting that, as the Rays had clearly sent messages about a circle that would come to be. I'd even been told that the circle's geometry would have something to do with Metatron's cube. Perhaps it would even fall after we left Wiltshire, as Keir and I were to leave August 11, one week before the sign in the fields of West Kennett indicating something occurring on August 17.

We went armed with video and still cameras out to the ridgeway, as this was daytime and I was thinking about acquiring some good footage to share with audiences for my presentations. We climbed over the barbed wire fence and on to the tumali now patrolled by the biggest cows I've ever seen.

Reaching the top, Keir went to put the video camera on a tripod, and he was suddenly surrounded by a swarm of small flies. He panicked and yelled to me to do something quickly. I began to say prayers, and he shouted to me that he thought all he had to do was put the camera down. And the instant he did, the flies withdrew and swarmed around me. They left me too, as soon as I put my camera on the ground. Then a few moments later, they were back on Keir. Confused, he reached into his back pocket and said, "Oh my God Mom, I'm packing!" and he took a disposable camera out of his jeans. The flies retreated immediately. What an event this had been!

Clearly we were not meant to photograph anything up there, which I took as a sign that the Universal forces had already been summoned and perhaps the energies were already gathering to create a circle. That energy may have been caught by our cameras, which is clearly verboten to be taken by me or my lineage. It was odd indeed. I couldn't help but wonder whether a bird or an insect actually understands that God uses them as active participants in delivering their messages. Did that bird that screamed at us at West Kennett have a commission to do that? How far ahead are these things planned? After all, Jodi had been told months before to look up. Was it a casual request from the Universe or a mandate? Did God say, by the way if you're in the vicinity of . . . would you mind yelling at. . . . Maybe these animals were actually shape shifted ECs? Derek can shape shift into anything, so why not an Extra Celestial? Lots of questions remained as the animal totems multiplied.

A man appeared far off in the distance, and he was pointing to the wheat field below and directly in front of us. I pointed out that it looked like Derek, and Keir agreed. Then the man disappeared and reappeared with a horse and rider along with him. Keir asked what a horse and rider meant, and I heard "Destiny." The man, the horse, and rider continued to appear and disappear in the distance. Keir and I were both unsure of what we were seeing. Were they real humans, or were we slipping in and out of some other reality?

Meanwhile, seven sheep marched out on the ridgeway in front of us noisily announcing their presence. Keir pointed out that the leader was a child, a lamb followed by its mom behind it. The sheep sat down all in a row overlooking the wheat field in front of us. We sat down in the tall grass overlooking the sheep that were looking over the field. "What is going on?" I asked, hoping for a direct answer from my favorite Light Beings.

Then I heard "At the end of three you will see a good example of sacred geometry in a field below thee." "How do I activate the field," I asked. "Prema Agni, Prema Agni, Prema Agni!" (The Fire of Divine Love). So I blessed the field with a Prema Agni. At that point, the sheep all got up and marched quietly back down the hill, and we left all excited. What an array of animal messengers we'd seen! Now all we had to do was wait three days and there would be a crop circle there! But when would we come back to see it and would the circle makers let us watch them create it?

A few days later, August 3, was the exact date of the Rays' and my third anniversary. So Keir and I decided to go back to Smeathe's Ridge on the three—the 3rd of August—even though it wasn't three full days since the arrival of their message. We agreed that this was the time those clever Rays were referring to, so we set out for the ridgeway in the late evening.

The week before Keir's arrival was marked by periodic visits of a ship of light outside my window. The vehicle took the form of the brightest of white light, which then split into rays of blue and morphed into a bigger Mandela of white lights that emitted beams of energy at my throat and third eye. The ECs had allowed Keir to see this vehicle, and that night we followed the ship of light up to Smeathe's Ridge where it played in the sky turning different colors and emitting rays of light in the star-filled sky.

Neither one of us was comfortable with the presence of a herd of tremendous cows in the middle of the night. They didn't looked thrilled to move out of the way for us. We were especially intimidated when they were behind us and all we could hear was their snorting. We hoped we hadn't pissed off any bulls! Clearly I needed to learn how to send cows more love than fear at night.

Way out on the ridgeway, the ECs showed themselves in the form of a multicolored UFO. And Keir was learning to distinguish between the real UFOs and the simple earthly illuminations next to them—one of their favorite games. How those Light Beings love to mimic lights! The beauty of the land at night was an extraordinary experience, especially for New Yorkers. But we'd acquired only one sleeping bag that wasn't big enough to accommodate both of us, and we left about 3 a.m.

The following day Keir took off from Smeathe's Ridge, and thinking that perhaps more activation of the land was needed, I took some friends and we did ceremony atop the tumali there, devouring all the chocolate we could eat. It had been almost three days now, and I was beginning to think that the Universe was playing with me.

The morning of the 5th of August was the very end of a total of three days, so Keir and I went back to the ridgeway overlooking the same glyph-less field where we'd done intention all that week. A large hare, the biggest bunny we'd ever seen, appeared on the road right beneath us, and Keir asked the meaning of a rabbit. I heard "Don't jump to conclusions." At that moment, I got angry and Keir had become impatient. Then I heard "Nan-see, you will see, a design in front of thee. Everything is yet to be."

I had never doubted anything they had ever told me, but I really couldn't understand the messages I was receiving. I felt frustrated and upset that whatever they were trying to tell me I wasn't able to figure out. I felt hopelessly attached to the outcome of a circle in the field below me and frustrated that all my issues of trust had surfaced. In response to my anger a few hours later I heard, "We see how it was mean to thee. We see what you mean. Forgive Thee?"

Of course I forgave them, but all the messages I'd ever received had been in truth and integrity. I still wasn't certain what they were saying as the pieces weren't connecting. I was leaving for Derek's center soon, and I doubted my ability to decipher the messages and understand their communications to me. Where was my trust, both in them and in me? Still, I kept hearing "One is there for all to see. The circle is yet to be."

Then one night within my sleep a circle did appear to me. It was a simple circle containing a cross. Sketching it out, I wondered about the origin of that particular cross and its meaning.

I spent my last night in Wiltshire with a friend on the top of the tumali at Smeathe's Ridge. This time, both of us were equipped with sleeping bags. My friend Catherine brought crystal bowls and when she played them, every one of those enormous cows lined up beside her to listen. That was definitely the way to a cow's heart in the middle of the night!

We watched as the usual array of phenomena surrounded us, and a stream of blue/white light appeared from a light far off in the distance penetrating my face in a transmission of grace from the Rays. I remembered, seven years before, that this same phenomenon had occurred at Camelot Castle Hotel that overlooks the sea (Tintagel, Cornwall). It was there that the first brilliant white light had appeared in front of me and I had awakened Keir to confirm its reality. Until that

Derek O'Neill, © 2007

moment, I hadn't realized that my journey with the ECs began even before I ever entered a field of wheat.

The opportunity to spend the entire night there on the land and to watch the morning fall on Mother Earth, regardless of the circle-less land beneath, was wondrous to me. The mist shifted quietly with the wind, as an orchestra of bird songs came from the patch of land called Smeathe's plantation directly below us. I had forgotten the glory of the Earth Mother as she begins anew each morning. "Start the day with Love, Spend the day with Love, End the day with Love" is what both Derek and Sai Baba say. I let go of the circle which was "yet to be." Wherever it was, however it looked, I let it go, surrendering it to the bigger picture, the healing of our precious planet we all hope to see.

I flew to Ireland later that day to stay at Creacon Lodge, Derek O'Neill's new healing center at Wexford. I'd come along with thirty-five others for his week-long-teacher-training course and initiation that would enable me to facilitate More Truth Will Set You Free Workshops of my own, with Derek overshadowing. His first comment to me as I got off the bus was, "You know there are wheat fields all around here," and he flashed me that leprechaun smile of his that means he's up to something.

Oh, God, here we go again, I thought. Just when I thought I'd left all the wheat fields and possibilities of circles behind me, they'd followed me to Ireland! Later that day, Derek showed me a wheat field right in back of the lodge and pointed to yet another—both fields adjacent to Nancy Lane—which of course sounded promising. Looking over the field he said, "See the etheric circle that's there?" I told him I couldn't see it, but that I'd been shown a pattern etherically in England. "Give it energy," he said, "and perhaps by the end of the week it will manifest physically." The bait had been set.

That first night at Creacon, I awoke to a blue flashing light, one of my roommate's cell phones that the Rays had taken over as a signaling device at the end of my bed. It had become a Mandela of brilliant blue flashing light poised in front of me. "Get up and get dressed," they said. "I don't want to wake the others," I said. "You won't." And they were right. No one woke up.

I fumbled for a few layers of clothes, as it was cold. I went outside and passed a light sensor on one of the buildings, which lit up as I walked by, startling me. I was anxious for what was next. Arriving at the parking lot, I was greeted with flashing lights inside the cars as I stood between them in total confusion—watching the lights go on and off—not realizing the difference between a light sensor and an EC. By this time, I was quietly asking the Rays what I was doing out here in the parking lot in the middle of the night. And if I was going to be beamed up, could they please do it quickly, because I was cold. Between the motion detectors and the car sensors there were flashing lights all over the place and at that moment, I was tired of the Universe's game of life with me. I could feel their laughter overhead, and I knew they thought this was hilarious. I figured Derek was really enjoying this too.

He was probably up in his room laughing his head off! What were the chances he didn't know I'd left my room and was outside?

I didn't receive an explanation until I went back to my room. "This was our way of telling thee that a crop circle was made for thee—a circle for all to see." I asked, "Is it here (in Ireland) or there (in England)?" "It is everywhere." This one, my intuition told me, could be a reference to the internet.

Spending the week at Creacon Lodge felt like every cell in my body was being refueled with the purest of Love and every moment an opportunity to experience the joy of simply being. The food is filled with an abundance of loving energy, as Derek blesses each morsel prepared, and Mary, the chef, caters to each guest's specific needs. The Irish Swami had wrapped us in blankets of God's Love, and Linda tucked us in tenderly. The roses in the garden really do carry the scent of heaven, and Derek invited us to drink the nectar of their dew each morning. That was an invitation to bliss out early in the day, and love unconditionally. It was going to be hard to leave this place.

The week passed by with all the grace and periodic uneasiness that accompanies Derek's Christed energy. It's the roller coaster ride of conscious understanding enabling its participants to move forward, leaving the patterns of the past behind. As teachers, we must do our own work and be as clear as humanly possible in order to facilitate others in their growth.

During breaks in the teachings, I would dutifully visit the fields adjacent to Nancy Lane and another across the way that Derek also suggested I visit. It was very wet weather that week, and by Thursday, Derek commented that sometimes these things manifest in the material plane and sometimes not.

As the week in Ireland progressed, I followed the circles of Wiltshire on the internet. The "croppies" were all waiting for one last circle of the summer—the last one seemingly a visual culmination of the summer's theme. When I checked late in the day on August 17, a gorgeous example of sacred geometry had landed at West Overton field. How ironic, I thought, as this was the field where it had all begun for us. It was the field that had, in 2003, held a simple "key" circle that had been called The Hand of God. Our giddy group that included Jodi,

Isabelle, Keir, and me had made intention and sound there till midnight, and by the time the sun came up, the circle had been extended the entire length of the field. (See page 78 for the photo of the extended crop circle at West Overton.) It was our first collaborative effort with the Universal forces that I am now privileged to know as my sacred family of ECs.

And then, a year later, in the summer of 2004, Jodi, Meryl, Keir, my friends, and I had gone back to the same field at West Overton, because I had intuited to go back to where we had been before. Jodi had activated the field with tone, we'd all giggled dutifully, and as we left that night, she'd gotten a message that there would be a circle there in three. Three days later, a circle did manifest in that very field. It was a simple snake that the farmer cut immediately. Our group had gone to videotape its remains that very day. It seemed to us that the farmer had been the snake!

Meanwhile I was sitting in Ireland unsure I could trust the messages that were coming to me. I was suffering from human confusion. There had been three entire years of messages of absolute integrity from the Rays. So where was the glyph they kept promising me? Smeathe's Ridge had gone yet another summer without a crop circle, and I had, once again, become attached to that outcome. Perhaps I was just supposed to surrender any part of me holding on to any aspect of disbelief.

Then, after Derek's initiation on August 17, I heard, "Nan-see, a circle has been made for thee. It's only landed etherically. It lies inside of thee." Well of course, that all made sense! August 17 was the date of the glyph's message at West Kennett. I had just been initiated to do the More Truth Workshops that very day! And as a facilitator, had I not chosen to carry within me the truth of Christ-consciousness, the truth that would set us all free?

I looked again at the windows above the café at Creacon, the windows we'd been told dated from the Knights Templar. I realized they bore the same cross that I'd been shown in my sleep! Of course! It was the Templar cross that was shown to me. There we were, all thirty six of us, the new Knights Templar of the Prema Agni, passing on the lineage of Christ-consciousness through the teachings of how to be. My relationship with the ECs is as complex and multi-leveled as any. Sometimes we get what we want from God and sometimes we get what we need to fulfill our mission, without attachment and without reaching for the fruits of our intuition.

I stayed in Dublin to catch a flight home August 20. It felt good to have some time to integrate the new energies within me. As I packed up my laptop for the flight home, the new circle, the one that had landed at West Overton popped up. It was the last thing I had seen on the internet a few days earlier, yet here it was again. That was strange. I hadn't used the internet for a couple of days. I took a moment to admire the circle's complex geometries. Beautiful—and somehow familiar.

By the time my plane landed I had unraveled the mystery. The circle at West Overton field was the one I had thought all along would land at Smeathe's Ridge. They'd landed the circle, but not in the place where I thought it would be. Instead they'd placed it back at where we'd begun, bringing us full circle!

I understood in that moment that the circle the Rays had shown me from their ship was likely this one. I might have recognized the terrain as we flew by—in future time—but I didn't quite get what and where they were showing me. They were playing!

It had landed on August 17 when the Saturn/Sun/Venus were conjunct just as the circle at West Kennett had specified. It had fallen in three, that is, three years since we last activated that field. It was at West Overton, which is located miles below Smeathe's Ridge. And it was most definitely an outstanding interpretation of Metatron's cube; a combination of all the platonic solids that comprise sacred geometry. Not only that, but it was a magnificent example of "Keetsoff Moran," the expression the Rays had used that translated means, "the flowering of the life of man."

The night of August 6, 2003, at West Overton field had been our very first communication with the circle makers. That moment was marked astrologically by the presence of a powerful Sun/Venus/Jupiter conjunction at exactly the same degree of the zodiac as the Sun/Venus/Saturn conjunction marked by the message in the field at West Kennett, and later manifesting in a breathtaking circle at West Overton at that same time, August 17, 2007. It was a four-year journey that started in a crop formation at West Overton field on August 6, 2003, and ended in the exact field four years later, coming full circle with accompanying twin astrology.

The circle that closed the circle at West Overton field, August 17, 2007. It was based on both Metatron's Cube and "Keetsoff Moran" or "the flowering of the life of man," © 2007 Steve Alexander

Jupiter brings expansion when the sun sheds its light on Love through wisdom and truth, while Saturn teaches us what we need to know to move through our journey. The ECs said, "Closing the circle that started in 2003 is the Oneness now revealed that we can all evolve to be."

I thought about all the ingratitude I'd been expressing over the past few weeks. It was so . . . human! The ECs had led me in a circle, and that circle was as intricately woven as the wheat itself. They said, "When I accepted the circle inside of me is when the truth came to me."

My first night in my own bedroom vortex I awoke to a sound in my ears that was so loud I couldn't imagine what the Rays were thinking. It was a high-pitched sound that had other, lower overtones. I asked them to turn it down, and I asked for an explanation of what it was I was hearing. Their reply was "Our way of congratulating thee for finding the sacred geometry. It's all within, you see, the sacred geometry of Thee. It's the sound of you and Thee! The design and the sound are the same and same is the name of the game. Throughout and within of Jesus C, (See!) Thou are a part of Thee."

The Game of Life

When those who have sat in my presentations or read this book call in the Rays or ECs to photograph, usually one or two blue balls of light appear, as the orbs seem to honor the will of the higher echelon of EC energies.

When last in Ireland, Derek told me about a conversation that he had with my mother, who is thinking about coming back in a human body. "She's thinking about coming back as one of Keir's children." That will provide an interesting new level of poignancy to grand-parenting.

Mother Mary, represented by my little glow-in-the-dark statuette, still serves as the perfect feminine compliment to the Rays' more masculine nature.

And now I, too, can activate Mary to turn blue, just by simply holding her in my hand when she's lit.

I've also heard "Because this book has come to be, a part of you and a part of Thee, so, too, your lineage will be, part of the miracle that's meant to be. Keir will inherit your channel to Thee!"

When writing these pages, my hand is overlaid with a sphere of the most beautiful blue light gliding along in this collaboration, symbolic of the physical union between God and human.

The Rays are the data base for our knowledge within, and the connection to them constitutes nothing less than our unification with the Universal force of the I Am Presence. Our invitation from the ECs is a leap of faith forward to the Divine embrace of full conscious awareness. They are the very best of teachers, always egoless, always appropriate and always willing to laugh and dance at the game of life. Unlike our human teachers, we can't put them on pedestals. Yet together we stand far taller than before.

What we do in one act of kindness, one loving gesture, or one loving moment of generosity can remake the world. When even one less judgment or complaint per day makes a difference in our human destiny, it is time for us to create new human choices. As the amount of light in our bodies grows, the light being in all of us develops, nurtured by our love for all God's creatures and our gratitude for all. And perhaps this is the way that mankind will evolve, as we move closer to the ancestral light that emanates through our celestial lineage.

With the Universe as choreographer, Jesus, Mary, Quan Yin, and Ganesh still perform to the rhythmic orchestration of energies here in my loft.

The Rays, as they say, "Are me and we are Thee." They are a part of my heart that is cherished as much as my son and my God. The lessons that have been received have been multi-leveled, like the flow chart of all memories collapsed through the funnel of life experience. The funnel cascades down into the vortex of words that have become this book. My lineage as well as the Masters and all other humans converge into the predetermined legacy of mankind, which has unfolded since the beginning of time.

Will the murmurings in my bedroom that I've recorded in this book be enough to make an impact on the understanding of our shared lineage? I'm still awestruck by the reality of the bluest of spheres that I witness day and night. God is no longer unseen when one can see God's messengers. The Universe has many faces, but only one familial soul.

While the Masters sit over our collective shoulders watching the Divine plan's script unfold, each of us has our own angelic guidance to support us. To access the purest gifts from the highest realms requires tuning into the messages that emerge from our human hearts. It is the continual vibration of the one eternal resonance undulating through the Universe, delivering the reminder to love.

For whatever choices we have made, there may be better ones we can create, as now is the time to ask for guidance in healing ourselves, as well as the Earth. This is the EC's Divine invitation to us, a gift from our lineage. It costs nothing more than the daily challenge to open our hearts. As the Rays said recently,

"We're all just here to have a good time, so if you hear a voice within you that says, have a good time, just say . . . 'Thanks, I am.'

Life's a game, play it."

EPILOGUE

A Note, with Love from your celestial family of Light:

When we begin to see (what Nan-see calls Metaphotography) photos of ECs, starting with the orbs, these images become a part of our collective consciousness or world brain.

The more photos that appear and the more we see them, the more they become a part of what we are.

Acceptance is the key. Our future is paved with the visual proof that shows that God is here at our doorstep. The more images seen, the more humankind will accept that the mind of man and the heart of man are One. In truth we have only to look within, but what we see and the record of what we can see will become a part of who we are. That coming together of what we see and what we know will be the turning point as the photos are all portals to conscious awareness. We must begin to believe what we can see. The more we believe what we see, the better off we will be!

We are all family and that is the point. Earth and sky are One. We love you so much, and the Universe expresses Love, in the mindfulness of knowing. That knowledge is nothing less than the power of Love, and the power of Love is the greatest force in the Universe. Our Love for humans is immeasurable—greater than the mass of the sun and moon combined and more than the vastness of space itself. Stay in the truth of your open hearts. We are here with loving support to guide you on your path.

ABOUT THE AUTHOR

Nancy Burson's work is shown in museums and galleries internationally including major exhibitions at The International Center of Photography and the New Museum in New York City, The Venice Biennale, The Contemporary Arts Museum in Houston, and The Museum of Contemporary Photography in Chicago. "Seeing and Believing," her traveling 2002 retrospective originating at the Grey Art Gallery, was nominated for Best Solo Museum Show of the Year in New York City by the International Association of Art Critics. She has served as a visiting professor at Harvard and was a member of the adjunct photography faculty at New York University's Tisch School of the Arts.

Burson is best known for her pioneering work in morphing technology, which age enhances the human face, enabling law enforcement officials to locate missing children and adults. Her Human Race Machine, which allows people to view themselves as a different race, was featured on Oprah in 2006. Currently there are Human Race Machines touring the U.S. college and university market as a diversity tool that provides students with the profound visual experience of being another race.

In the last few years she has collaborated with Creative Time, the Lower Manhattan Cultural Council, and Deutsche Bank in completing several important public art projects in New York City. These projects include the billboard "There's No Gene For Race" and the poster/postcard project "Focus on Peace." The LMCC's "Focus on Peace" project distributed 30,000 postcards and 7,000 posters around the site of the World Trade Center to coincide with the first anniversary of 9/11. Burson's first text-based book, *Focus: How Your Energy Can Change the World*, was published in 2004, and she has authored four books of her photography. As a photographer, writer, inventor, healer, and minister, Burson lectures and teaches worldwide, providing firsthand experience with the unseen.

Currently Burson is conducting periodic Evening Presentations and workshops to familiarize her audience with the material and phenomena included in this book.

For more information on *Lineage* visit: www.nancyburson.com